DEVELOPING NOTES FOR COMPETITIVE EXAMS

(JEE, NEET ,CUET ,UPSC, ICAR, JET, NDA, NTSE, KVPY ETC.)

ACHARYA VISHVENDRA

Made with ♥ on the Notion Press Platform
www.notionpress.com

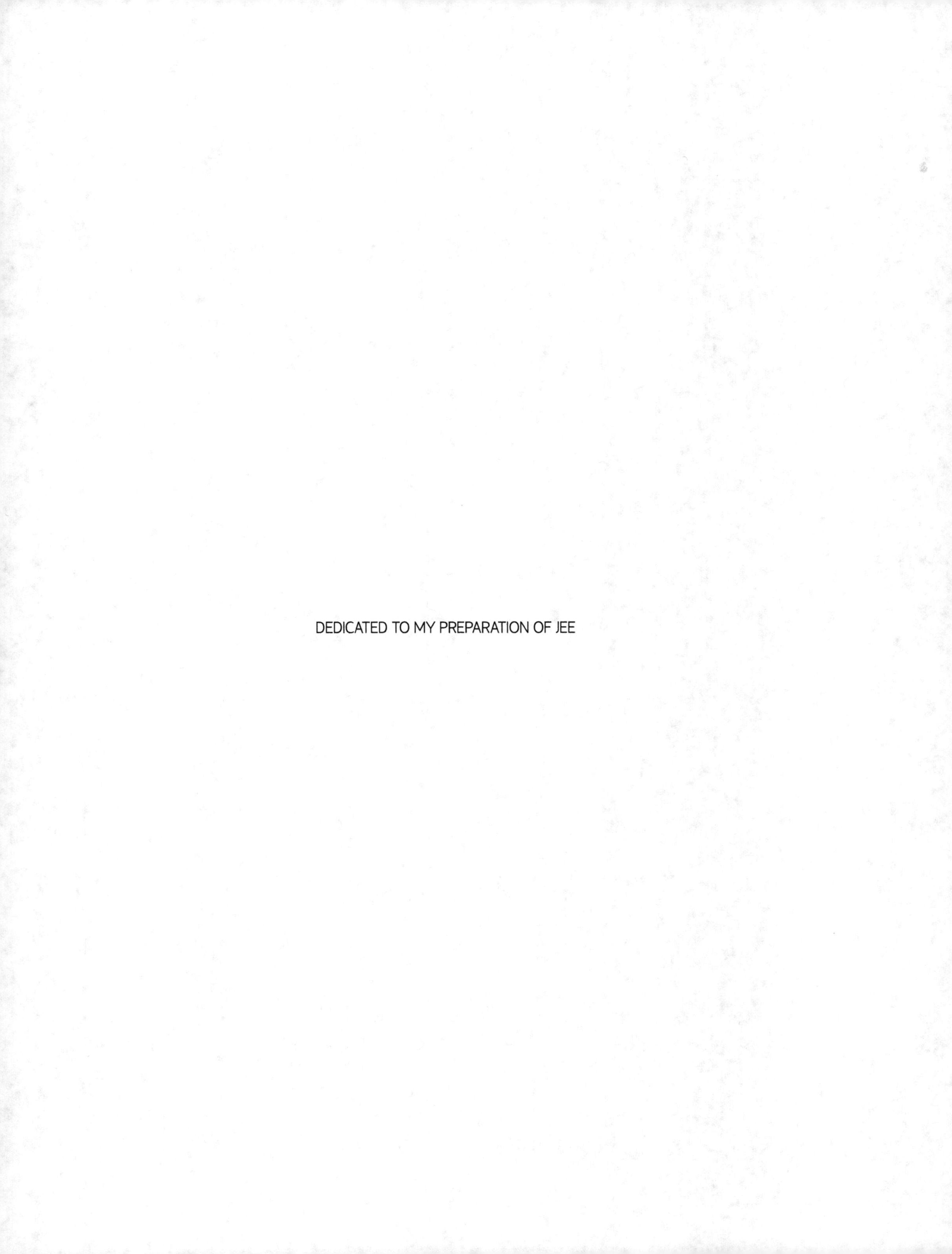

DEDICATED TO MY PREPARATION OF JEE

Contents

Foreword — vii

Preface — ix

Acknowledgements — xi

Prologue — xiii

1. Introduction — 1

2. Exam Pattern — 7

3. Detailed Syllabus — 21

4. Topicwise Analysis — 42

5. Previous Years Question Analysis — 51

6. Detailed Notes — 54

7. Short Notes — 56

8. Mind Maps — 68

9. Conclusions — 70

Write To Us: — 71

Foreword

Having detailed information about competitive exams at micro & macro level is the foundation step for success in competitive exam **(JEE, NEET, UPSC, CUET, NDA, NTSE, KVPY,ICAR, JET)** .Any competitive exam can be analysed as a system of 3 fundamental dimensions-

1.Information

2.Process

3.Energy

information is the first & most important dimension concerned with the preparation of competitive exams**(JEE, NEET, UPSC, CUET, NDA, NTSE, KVPY,ICAR, JET)**

I have observed my own preparation for jee & that of thousands of my students during my working as a physics faculty in reputed coaching institutes of kota & delhi.and i have decoded that optimal information source is extremly important for competitive exams.specially the pattern,weightage & analysis of last years questions ensures optimal preparation for competitive exams.

This book is an effort to provide optimal information source to the students preparing for competitive exams.so that they can be more advanced and focused for their preparation.

Preface

Proper management of information is crucial for cracking competitive exam**(JEE, NEET, UPSC, CUET, NDA, NTSE, KVPY,ICAR, JET Etc)**.This book is an effort to guide students for developing well structured,concise & comprehensive notes for cracking competitive exams.

This book contains information varying from macro level to microlevel which are required to crack competitive exams**((JEE, NEET, UPSC, CUET, NDA, NTSE, KVPY,ICAR, JET Etc)**

Acknowledgements

Thanks to my teachers,students & critics to stimulate me for doing a fundamental work for solving the problems which i faced during my JEE preparation.

Prologue

Having a well structured information is a backbone of success in competitive exams.This book contains about every information related to competitive exams**(JEE, NEET, UPSC, CUET, NDA, NTSE, KVPY,ICAR, JET Etc)**

CHAPTER ONE

INTRODUCTION

1.1:INTRODUCTION:

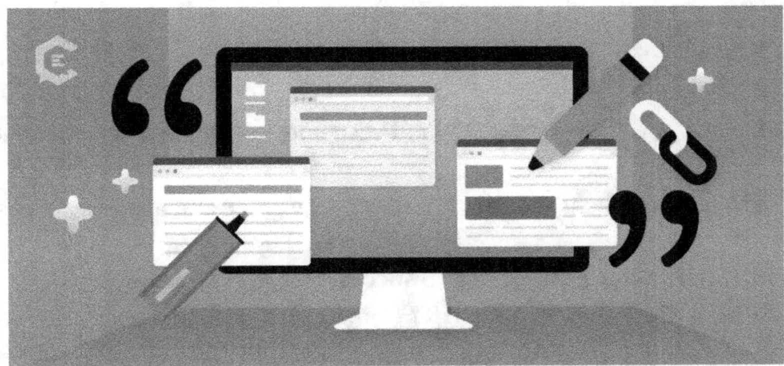

FIG-1:CONCISE & COMPREHENSIVE INFORMATION SOURCE

Having concise & comprehensive information is the fundamental requirement to crack a competitive exam.As the syllabus is extremly wide,so its necessary to know what to study?revise that again & again & practice its manipulations in all possible orders.

This book contains elaborative information source at macro & micro level for several competitive exams((**JEE, NEET, UPSC, CUET, NDA, NTSE, KVPY,ICAR, JET Etc)** held in our country

FIG-2:VARIOUS COMPETITIVE EXAMS IN INDIA

1.2:WHY OPTIMISED INFORMATION SOURCE IS NECESSARY?

FIG-3:WHY OPTIMISED INFORMATION SOURCE IS NECESSARY?

Universe is guided by rigid protocols.just decode the rules of the game and achieve success.without decoding rules you can't win.

so havinG optimised information source is crucial to success.

1.3:WHY COMPETITIVE EXAMS ARE NECESSARY?

competitive exams are meant not only to judge your talent but also to test your management,planning & performance skills. Any competitive exam is designed to check the functionalities of your "MIND-BRAIN SYSTEM".

As you must have realised that we have a habit of **self boasting**.we are internally **somewhat less than** what we project on the **outside world.**

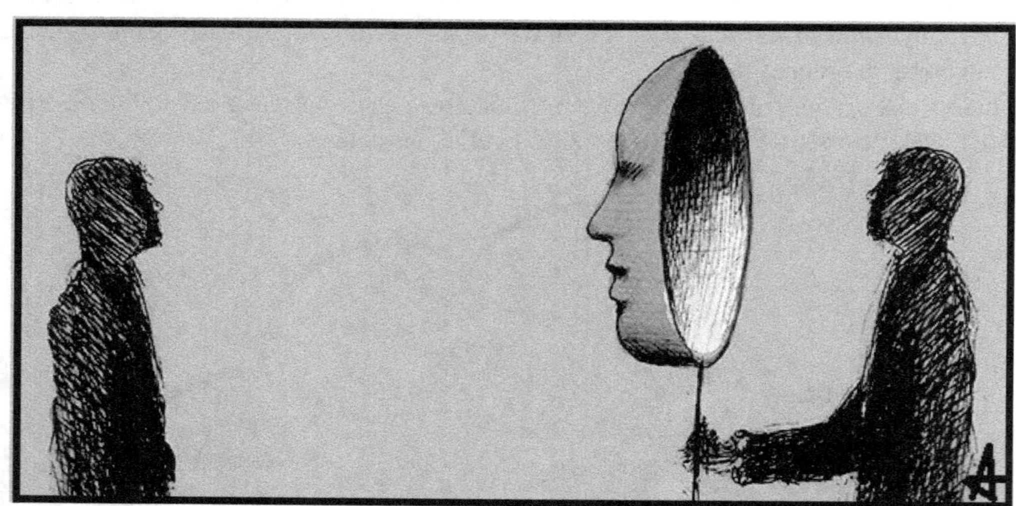

FIG-4:WE ARE DIFFERENT FROM WHAT WE PROJECT

So there has to be a **well structured,scientific & systematic mechanism** to find the **real person** behind the fake mask.so **competitive exams** are the **mechanisms** to decode the **reality of a person** based on his **neural capabilities** along with his **will power.**

Most of the students have an underdeveloped"**MIND-BRAIN SYSTEM**" due to poor **training & learning.**They have just worked on their temporary memory which is the second layer of human "**MIND-BRAIN SYSTEM**"and is just to make you survive.

if we think beyond survival,we have to cross the boundaries of temporary memory and have to access permanent memory.This process requires a systematic approach and can be achieved by proper **training programs.**

if you feel that you are unable to perform better in your exam because of inability to access your **permanent memory** then you can refer to the book "OST-DEVELOPING MIND,DEVELOP INDIA"

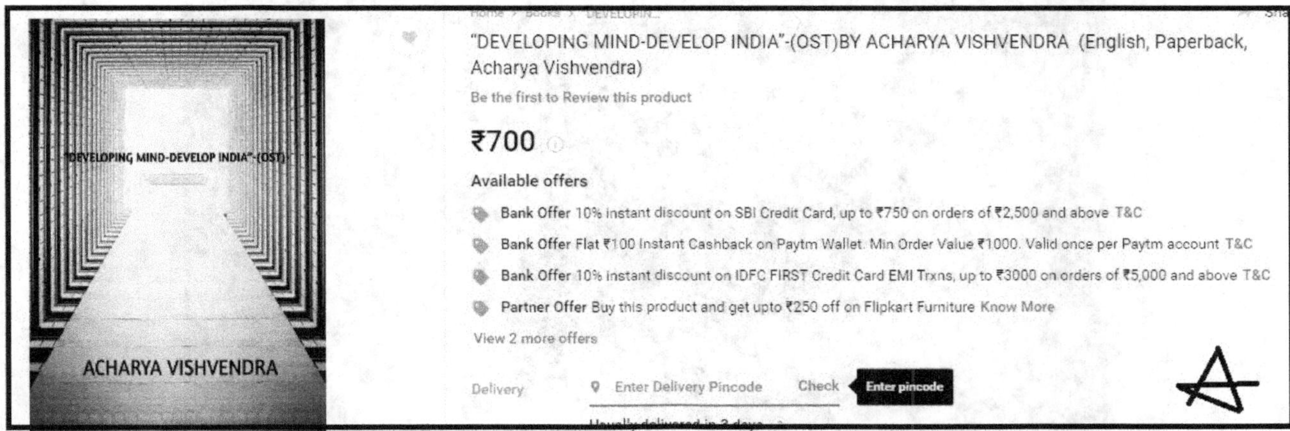

FIG-5:DEVELOPING MIND,DEVELOP INDIA

competition exams are getting advanced day by day as per the need of the society for being more and more comfortable and hence the entry in good colleges is not everybody's cup of tea. it requires a well developed "MIND-BRAIN SYSTEM" to decode **competitive exams** and getting entry into a good college.

For instance,In 2018, around 11.5 lakh students registered for JEE Main and 2,31,024 students qualified for JEE Advanced and at the end only 31,988 (that too after the revised cut-off) students qualified JEE Advanced. These candidates will fight for 11,279 seats available in the IITs in India.

To prepare themself for the challenging path, sudents are required to work on their "MIND-BRAIN SYSTEM" at very early age. Students should start appearing in various national and international-level competitive exams at very early age so that their "MIND-BRAIN SYSTEM" starts developing and can learn **advanced functions** as early as possible.

1.4:ADVANTAGES OF COMPETITIVE EXAMS:

Exposure to **competitive exams** improves **learning** and builds **self-confidence** and develops **problem solving sillls** which develops the "MIND-BRAIN SYSTEM" of the students and help them perform better in life.

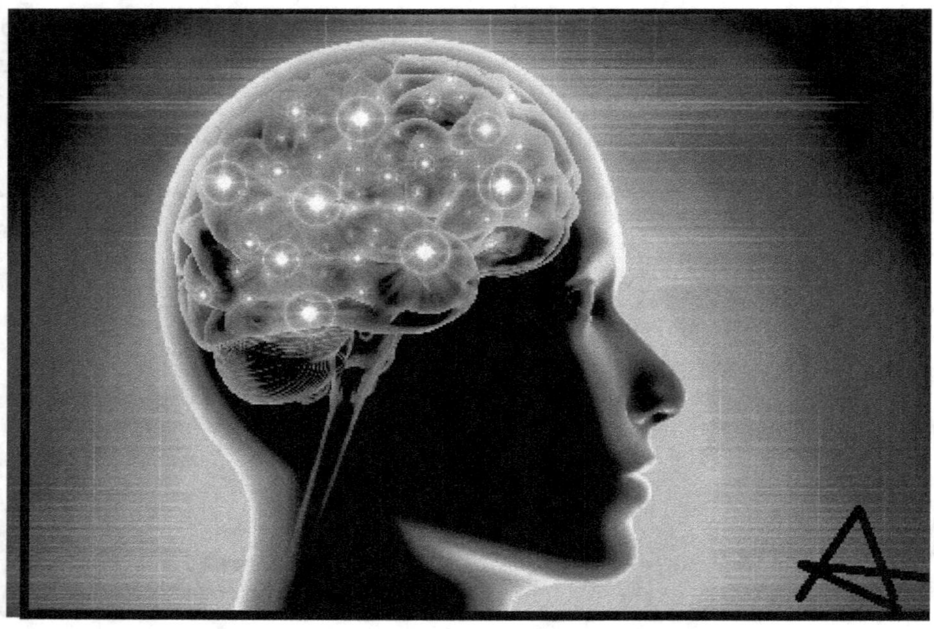

FIG-6:BETTER MIND-BRAIN SYSTEM

They explore the opportunities to enter foreign universities including worldwide number 1 university, MIT. Medallists in **International Olympiads** have a fair chance of getting into **top-class foreign universities** compared to others. There are reservations in Few colleges have reserved seats for such scholars.

FIG-7:MIT

These exams also help out in choosing a career as students start identifying their areas of interest while getting a deeper knowledge of subjects.Awards, rewards and scholarships not only provide financial assistance in further studies but also boost morale while moving ahead in the future.

FIG-8:COMPETITIVE EXAMS ARE ROADS TO BETTER FUTURE

hence it can be concluded that there are **no disadvantages** of appearing for such **competitive exams** and it's just a myth that they can hamper **regular studies**. An early step will articulate your journey of success.

1.5:STRATEGIES FOR PREPARATION OF COMPETITIVE EXAMS:

FIG-9: STRATEGIES FOR COMPETITIVE EXAMS

competitive exams are meant to check you in **multi-dimensional aspects of problem solving skills,will power,determination,plannning etc.**

FIG-10: PROBLEM SOLVING SKILLS

hence the traditional method of **studying for long hours**, having room filled with a lot of **competitive books** around the study table, cutting aloof with the surrounding, and many more such ideas will not work.Now its the time to prepare with a strategy,have a detailed notes of what is being **asked in the exam**,making **mind-maps,revising the patterns** again and again.Use **mental simulation techniques to adapt** to the high **pressure exam conditions** are now the required key fieldS.

some of the **strategies** which may be used are:

1.Have a concise & comprehensive syllabus:

2.Have detailed notes:

3.Make short notes:

4.Make Mind maps:

5.Have previous years question papers to decode the exam pattern:

6.use Mental simulation techniques to get adapted to the high pressure exam conditions:

CHAPTER TWO

EXAM PATTERN

3.1:At present there are many competitive exams in india for admissions to higher educations.These includes:

1.JEE MAIN 2.JEE ADVANCED 3.NEET 4.CUET 5.UPSC 6.NDA 7.ICAR 8.JET 9.NTSE 10.KVPY

3.2:EXAM PATTERN:

1.JEE ADVANCED:

FIG-11:JEE ADVANCED

JEE Advanced Paper 1 pattern (Same for Physics, Chemistry and Mathematics)

Section	Types of questions	No. of questions	Maximum Marks
Section 1	MCQs with Single Correct Option	6	18
Section 2	Single Correct Option	6	24
Section 3	Numerical Value Answer	6	24

JEE Advanced Paper 2 pattern (Same for Physics, Chemistry and Mathematics)

Section	Types of questions	No. of questions	Maximum Marks
Section 1	MCQs with one or more than one correct answer	6	24
Section 2	Numerical value answer type questions	6	24
Section 3	Single-digit integer answer (0-9)	6	18

FIG-12:JEE ADVANCED PATTERN

MARKING SCHEME FOR JEE ADVANCED PAPER-1

Section	Question Type	Total Questions	Full Marks	Partial Marks	Negative Marks	Maximum Marks
1	Single Correct Option	6	+3 If only the correct answer is selected	–	-1 (in all other cases)	18
2	One or more option (s) is correct	6	+4 – If the correct option(s) is selected	+3 – If all the four options are correct but only three options are chosen+2 – If three or more options are correct but only two options are chosen, both of which are correct options. +1 – If two or more options are correct but only one option is chosen and it is a correct option.	-2: In all other cases	24
3	Numerical Value Answer	6	+4 – If only the correct numerical value is entered	–	–	24

FIG-13:JEE ADVANCED PATTERN

Section	Question Type	Total Questions	Full Marks	Partial Marks	Negative Marks	Maximum Marks
1	MCQs with 4 options (one or more than one correct option)	6	+4 If only (all) the correct option(s) is (are) chosen	+3 If all the four options are correct but only three options are chosen +2 if three or more options are correct but only two options are chosen, both of the options must be correct +1 if two or more options are correct buy only one option is chosen and it must be correct	-2 (In all other cases)	24
2	Numerical value answer type questions	6	+4 if only correct numerical value is given			24
3	Single-digit integer answer (0-9)	6	+3 if only the correct integer is entered	–	-1 in all other cases	18

FIG-14:JEE ADVANCED PATTERN

2.JEE MAIN:

Paper	Subjects	Section A	Section B	Mode of the Examination	Timing of the Examination (IST) First Shift	Second Shift
JEE Main 2022 Exam Pattern						
Paper 1 (B.E./B.Tech.)	Mathematics	20*	10*	Computer Based Test (CBT) mode	09:00 a.m. to 12:00 p.m.	03:00 p.m. to 06:00 p.m.
	Physics	20*	10*			
	Chemistry	20*	10*			
	Total	90				
Paper 2A (B. Arch.)	Mathematics – Part I	20*	10*	Computer Based Test (CBT) mode except Drawing Test (Part-III) in pen and paper (offline) mode, to be attempted on drawing sheet of A4 size	09:00 a.m. to 12:00 p.m.	03:00 p.m. to 06:00 p.m.
	Aptitude Test – Part II	50				
	Drawing Test – Part III	02				
	Total	82				
Paper 2B (B. Planning)	Mathematics – Part I	20*	10*	Computer Based Test (CBT) mode	03:00 p.m. to 06:00 p.m.	
	Aptitude Test – Part II	50				
	Planning – Part III	25				
	Total	105				

* For Paper 1 and Part-I of Paper 2, each Subject will have **two sections.** Section A will be of Multiple-Choice Questions (MCQs) and Section B will contain Questions whose answers are to be filled in as a numerical value. In Section B, candidates have to attempt any **05 (five) questions out of 10.** There will be **negative marking for both Section A and Section B.** For each question in Section B, **enter the correct integer value** of the answer using the mouse and the on-screen virtual numeric keypad in the place designated to enter the answer. **For Section B, the answer should be rounded off to the nearest Integer.**

FIG-15:JEE MAIN PATTERN

3.NEET:

FIG-16:NEET

NEET 2022 Exam pattern – Section wise distribution			
Sl. No.	Subject	No. of Questions	Total Marks
1	Physics	Section A: 35 + Section B: 10 (15 provided, 10 to be answered) = 45	180
2	Chemistry	Section A: 35 + Section B: 10 (15 provided, 10 to be answered) = 45	180
4	Zoology	Section A: 35 + Section B: 10 (15 provided, 10 to be answered) = 45	180
3	Botany	Section A: 35 + Section B: 10 (15 provided, 10 to be answered) = 45	180
Total		180	720

FIG-17:NEET PATTERN

4.UPSC:

FIG-18:UPSC

Civils Exam Pattern – Prelims					
Paper	Type	No. of questions	UPSC Total Marks	Duration	Negative marks
General Studies I	Objective	100	200	2 hours	Yes
General Studies II (CSAT)	Objective	80	200	2 hours	Yes
Total UPSC marks for Prelims	400 (where GS Paper II is qualifying in nature with minimum qualifying marks fixed at 33%)				

FIG-19:UPSC PATTERN

UPSC CSE Exam Pattern – Mains			
Paper	Subject	Duration	IAS Total marks
Paper A	Compulsory Indian language	3 hours	300
Paper B	English	3 hours	300
Paper I	Essay	3 hours	250
Paper II	General Studies I	3 hours	250
Paper III	General Studies II	3 hours	250
Paper IV	General Studies III	3 hours	250
Paper V	General Studies IV	3 hours	250
Paper VI	Optional I	3 hours	250
Paper VII	Optional II	3 hours	250

FIG-20:UPSC PATTERN

5.CUET:

FIG-21:CUET

CUET Exam Pattern 2022				
Sections	Subjects/ Tests	No. of Questions	To be Attempted	Duration
Section IA	13 Languages	50	40 in each language	45 minutes for each language
Section IB	19 Languages			
Section II	27 Domain-specific Subjects	50	40	45 minutes for each subject
Section III	General Test	75	60	60 minutes

FIG-22:CUET PATTERN

6.NDA:

FIG-23:NDA

NDA General Ability Test	Sections	Maximum marks
Part A – English	–	200
Part B – General Awareness	Physics	100
	History, Freedom Movement, etc.	80
	Geography	80
	Chemistry	60
	General Science	40
	Current Events	40
	Total	600

FIG-24: NDA PATTERN

NDA – SSB Interview Pattern 2022		
Stage 1	Screening Test	1. Verbal and non-verbal tests. 2. PPDT
Stage 2	Psychological Test	1. Thematic Apperception Test (TAT) 2. Word Association Test (WAT) 3. Situation Reaction Test (SRT) 4. Self Description Test (SD)
	Group Testing Officers Test	1. GD 2. GPE 3. PGT 4. HGT 5. IOT 6. Command Task 7. Snake race/Group Obstacle Race 8. Individual lecture 9. FGT
	Personal Interview & conference	–

FIG-25: NDA PATTERN

7.ICAR:

FIG-26:ICAR

ICAR IARI Technician Exam Pattern 2022				
Paper/Section	Subject	No. of Questions	Max marks	Duration
I	General Knowledge	25	25	
II	Mathematics	25	25	
III	Science	25	25	1.5 hours
IV	Social Science	25	25	
Total		100	100	

FIG-27:ICAR PATTERNS

PATTERN OF ICAR 2022

The first and foremost step to begin with any preparation is to know the complete exam pattern for the exam. Here we have discussed the ICAR IARI Technician Exam Pattern 2022 for Computer Based Test (CBT).

Key points for ICAR IARI Technician Exam Pattern 2022 are as-

1. There will be 100 Objective Type- Multiple Choice Questions in CBT.

2. Each correct answer will be awarded 1 mark.

3. There is a negative marking of the ¼th mark (0.25) mark for each incorrect answer.

4. The total time duration for ICAR IARI CBT is 1.5 hours (90 minutes).

5. The CBT will be set in bilingual language (both in English & Hindi) for all the sections.

6. There will be 4 subjects- General Knowledge, Mathematics, Science and Social Science each holding equal weightage.

FIG-28:ICAR PATTERNS

8.NTSE

FIG-29:NTSE

NTSE Stage 1 Exam Pattern 2021-22

Paper	Number of questions	Maximum marks	Duration (Minutes)
MAT	100	100	120
SAT – Maths, Science and Social Science	100	100	120

FIG-30:NTSE PATTERN

NTSE Exam Pattern 2021-22 for Stage 2

Papers	Maximum Marks	Number of Questions	Time Allotted
MAT	100	100	120 minutes
SAT (Mathematics, Science, Social Sciences)	100	100	120 minutes

FIG-31:NTSE PATTERN

10.KVPY:

FIG-32:KVPY

Subjects	Total Questions in Part – I	Total Questions in Part – II	Total Marks
Mathematics	15	5	25
Physics	15	5	25
Chemistry	15	5	25
Biology	15	5	25
Total	60	20	100

FIG-33:KVPY PATTERN

KVPY SX paper pattern 2022

Below we have provided the KVPY SX/SB exam pattern for your reference:

Subjects	Total Questions in Part – I	Total Questions in Part – II	Total Marks
Mathematics	20	10	40
Physics	20	10	40
Chemistry	20	10	40
Biology	20	10	40
Total	80	40	160

FIG-34:KVPY PATTERN

CHAPTER THREE

DETAILED SYLLABUS

3.1: After being familiar with the exam pattern its very necessary to have a **concise and comprehensivesyllabus** of the exams.

3.2:DETAILED EXAM SYLLABUS:

FIG-35:DETAILED EXAM SYLLABUS

3.2.1: DETAILED SYLLABUS FOR JEE ADVANCED:

FIG-36:DETAILED SYLLABUS FOR JEE ADVANCED

3.2.1.1:PHYSICS

UNIT-1:INTRODUCTORY PHYSICS:

General Units and dimensions, dimensional analysis; least count, significant figures; Methods of measurement and error analysis for physical quantities pertaining to the following experiments: Experiments based on using Vernier calipers and screw gauge (micrometer), Determination of g using simple pendulum, Young's modulus - elasticity of the material Surface tension of water by capillary rise and effect of detergents. Specific heat of a liquid using calorimeter, focal length of a concave mirror and a convex lens using u-v method, Speed of sound using resonance column, Verification of Ohm's law using voltmeter and ammeter, and specific resistance of the material of a wire using meter bridge and post office box.

UNIT-2:MECHANICS

Kinematics in one and two dimensions (Cartesian coordinates only), projectiles; Uniform circular motion; Relative velocity.
Newton's laws of motion; Inertial and uniformly accelerated frames of reference; Static and dynamic friction; Kinetic and potential energy; Work and power; Conservation of linear momentum and mechanical energy.
Systems of particles; Centre of mass and its motion; Impulse; Elastic and inelastic collisions.
Rigid body, moment of inertia, parallel and perpendicular axes theorems, moment of inertia of uniform bodies with simple geometrical shapes; Angular momentum; Torque; Conservation of angular momentum; Dynamics of rigid bodies with fixed axis of rotation; Rolling without slipping of rings, cylinders and spheres; Equilibrium of rigid bodies; Collision of point masses with rigid bodies. Forced and damped oscillation (in one dimension), resonance.
Linear and angular simple harmonic motions.
Hooke's law, Young's modulus.
Law of gravitation; Gravitational potential and field; Acceleration due to gravity; Kepler's law, Geostationary orbits, Motion of planets and satellites in circular orbits; Escape velocity.
Pressure in a fluid; Pascal's law;Buoyancy; Surface energy and surface tension, angle of contact, drops, bubbles and capillary rise. Viscosity (Poiseuille's equation excluded), Modulus of rigidity and bulk modulus in mechanics. Stoke's law; Terminal velocity, Streamline flow, equation of continuity, Bernoulli's theorem and its applications. Wave motion (plane waves only), longitudinal and transverse waves, superposition of waves; Progressive and stationary waves; Vibration of strings and air columns; Resonance; Beats; Speed of sound in gases; Doppler effect (in sound)

UNIT-3:THERMAL PHYSICS

Thermal expansion of solids, liquids and gases; Calorimetry, latent heat; Heat conduction in one dimension; Elementary concepts of convection and radiation; Newton's law of cooling; Ideal gas laws; Specific heats (C_v and C_p for monoatomic and diatomic gases); Isothermal and adiabatic processes, bulk modulus of gases; Equivalence of heat and work; First law of thermodynamics and its applications (only for ideal gases); Second law of thermodynamics, reversible and irreversible processes, Carnot engine and its efficiency; Blackbody radiation: absorptive and emissive powers; Kirchhoff's law; Wien's displacement law, Stefan's law.

UNIT-4:ELECTROMAGNETISM

Coulomb's law; Electric field and potential; Electrical potential energy of a system of point charges and of electrical dipoles in a uniform electrostatic field; Electric field lines; Flux of electric field; Gauss's law and its application in simple cases, such as, to find field due to infinitely long straight wire, uniformly charged infinite plane sheet and uniformly charged thin spherical shell.
Capacitance; Parallel plate capacitor with and without dielectrics; Capacitors in series and parallel; Energy stored in a capacitor.
Electric current; Ohm's law; Series and parallel arrangements of resistances and cells; Kirchhoff's

laws and simple applications; Heating effect of current.

Biot–Savart's law and Ampere's law; Magnetic field near a current-carrying straight wire, along the axis of a circular coil and inside a long straight solenoid; Force on a moving charge and on a current-carrying wire in a uniform magnetic field.

Magnetic moment of a current loop; Effect of a uniform magnetic field on a current loop; Moving coil galvanometer, voltmeter, ammeter and their conversions.

Electromagnetic induction: Faraday's law, Lenz's law; Self and mutual inductance; RC, LR, LC and LCR(in series) circuits with d.c. and a.c. sources.

Electromagtic Waves

Electromagnetic waves and their characteristics. Electromagnetic spectrum (radio waves, microwaves, infrared, visible, ultraviolet, x-rays, gamma rays) including elementary facts about their uses.

UNIT-5:OPTICS

Rectilinear propagation of light; Reflection and refraction at plane and spherical surfaces; Total internal reflection; Deviation and dispersion of light by a prism; Thin lenses; Combinations of mirrors and thin lenses; Magnification.

Wave nature of light: Huygen's principle, interference limited to Young's double slit experiment. Diffraction due to a single slit. Polarization of light, plane polarized light; Brewster's law, Polaroids.

UNIT-6:MODERN PHYSICS

Atomic nucleus; α, β and γ radiations; Law of radioactive decay; Decay constant; Half-life and mean life; Binding energy and its calculation; Fission and fusion processes; Energy calculation in these processes.

Photoelectric effect; Bohr's theory of hydrogen-like atoms; Characteristic and continuous X-rays, Moseley's law; de Broglie wavelength of matter waves.

3.2.1.2:CHEMISTRY
PHYSICAL CHEMISTRY
UNIT1: MOLE CONCEPT

Concept of atoms and molecules; Dalton's atomic theory; Mole concept; Chemical formulae; Balanced chemical equations; Calculations (based on mole concept and stoichiometry) involving common oxidation-reduction, neutralisation, and displacement reactions; Concentration in terms of mole fraction, molarity, molality and normality.

UNIT-2: STATES OF MATTER

Gas laws and ideal gas equation, absolute scale of temperature; Deviation from ideality, van der Waals equation; Kinetic theory of gases, average, root mean square and most probable velocities and their relation with temperature; Law of partial pressures; Diffusion of gases. Intermolecular interactions: types, distance dependence, and their effect on properties; Liquids: vapour pressure, surface tension, viscosity.

UNIT-3: ATOMIC STRUCTURE

Bohr model, spectrum of hydrogen atom; Wave-particle duality, de Broglie hypothesis; Uncertainty principle; Qualitative quantum mechanical picture of hydrogen atom: Energies, quantum numbers, wave function and probability density (plots only), shapes of s, p and d orbitals; Aufbau principle; Pauli's exclusion principle and Hund's rule.

UNIT-4: CHEMICAL BONDING & MOLECULAR STRUCTURE

Orbital overlap and covalent bond; Hybridisation involving s, p and d orbitals only; Molecular orbital energy diagrams for homonuclear diatomic species (up to Ne2); Hydrogen bond; Polarity in molecules, dipole moment; VSEPR model and shapes of molecules (linear, angular, triangular, square planar, pyramidal, square pyramidal, trigonal bipyramidal, tetrahedral and octahedral).

UNIT-5: CHEMICAL THERMODYNAMICS

Intensive and extensive properties, state functions, First law of thermodynamics; Internal energy, work (pressure-volume only) and heat; Enthalpy, heat capacity, standard state, Hess's law; Enthalpy of reaction, fusion and vapourization, and lattice enthalpy; Second law of thermodynamics; Entropy; Gibbs energy; Criteria of equilibrium and spontaneity.

UNIT-6: CHEMICAL & IONIC EQUILIBRIUM

Law of mass action; Significance of and in chemical equilibrium; Equilibrium constant (Kp and Kc) and reaction quotient, Le Chatelier's principle (effect of concentration, temperature and pressure); Solubility product and its applications, common ion effect, pH and buffer solutions; Acids and bases (Bronsted and Lewis concepts); Hydrolysis of salts.

UNIT-7: ELECTROCHEMISTRY

Electrochemical cells and cell reactions; Standard electrode potentials; Electrochemical work, Nernst equation; Electrochemical series, emf of galvanic cells; Faraday's laws of electrolysis; Electrolytic conductance, specific, equivalent and molar conductivity, Kohlrausch's law; Batteries: Primary and Secondary, fuel cells; Corrosion.

UNIT-8: CHEMICAL KINETICS

Rates of chemical reactions; Order and molecularity of reactions; Rate law, rate constant, half-life; Differential and integrated rate expressions for zero and first order reactions; Temperature dependence of rate constant (Arrhenius equation and activation energy); Catalysis: Homogeneous and heterogeneous, activity and selectivity of solid catalysts, enzyme catalysis and its mechanism.

UNIT-9: SOLID STATE

Classification of solids, crystalline state, seven crystal systems (cell parameters a, b, c, α, β, γ), close packed structure of solids (cubic and hexagonal), packing in fcc, bcc and hcp lattices; Nearest neighbours, ionic radii and radius ratio, point defects.

UNIT-10: SOLUTIONS

Henry's law; Raoult's law; Ideal solutions; Colligative properties: lowering of vapour pressure, elevation of boiling point, depression of freezing point, and osmotic pressure; van't Hoff factor.

UNIT-11: SURFACE CHEMISTRY

Elementary concepts of adsorption: Physisorption and Chemisorption, Freundlich adsorption isotherm; Colloids: types, methods of preparation and general properties; Elementary ideas of emulsions, surfactants and micelles (only definitions and examples).

INORGANIC CHEMISTRY

UNIT1: CLASSIFICATION OF ELEMENTS & PERIODICITY IN PROPERTIES:

Modern periodic law and the present form of periodic table; electronic configuration of elements; periodic trends in atomic radius, ionic radius, ionization enthalpy, electron gain enthalpy, valence, oxidation states, electronegativity, and chemical reactivity.

UNIT-2: HYDROGEN

Position of hydrogen in periodic table, occurrence, isotopes, preparation, properties and uses of hydrogen; hydrides – ionic, covalent and interstitial; physical and chemical properties of water, heavy water; hydrogen peroxide-preparation, reactions, use and structure; hydrogen as a fuel.

UNIT-3: S BLOCK ELEMENTS

Alkali and alkaline earth metals-reactivity towards air, water, dihydrogen, halogens, acids; their reducing nature including solutions in liquid ammonia; uses of these elements; general characteristics of their oxides, hydroxides, halides, salts of oxoacids; anomalous behaviour of lithium and beryllium; preparation, properties, and uses of compounds of sodium (sodium carbonate, sodium chloride, sodium hydroxide, sodium hydrogen carbonate) and calcium (calcium oxide, calcium hydroxide, calcium carbonate, calcium sulphate).

UNIT-4: P-BLOCK ELEMENTS

Oxidation state and trends in chemical reactivity of elements of groups 13-17; anomalous properties of boron, carbon, nitrogen, oxygen, and fluorine with respect to other elements in their respective groups.

Group 13: Reactivity towards acids, alkalis, and halogens; preparation, properties, and uses of borax, orthoboric acid, diborane, boron trifluoride, aluminium chloride, and alums; uses of boron and aluminium.

Group 14: Reactivity towards water and halogen; allotropes of carbon and uses of carbon; preparation, properties, and uses of carbon monoxide, carbon dioxide, silicon dioxide, silicones, silicates, zeolites.

Group 15: Reactivity towards hydrogen, oxygen, and halogen; allotropes of phosphorous; preparation, properties, and uses of dinitrogen, ammonia, nitric acid, phosphine, phosphorus trichloride, phosphorus pentachloride; oxides of nitrogen and oxoacids of phosphorus.

Group 16: Reactivity towards hydrogen, oxygen, and halogen; simple oxides; allotropes of sulfur; preparation/manufacture, properties, and uses of dioxygen, ozone, sulfur dioxide, sulfuric acid; oxoacids of sulfur.

Group 17: Reactivity towards hydrogen, oxygen, and metals; preparation/manufacture, properties, and uses of chlorine, hydrogen chloride and interhalogen compounds; oxoacids of halogens, bleaching powder.

Group 18: Chemical properties and uses; compounds of xenon with fluorine and oxygen.

UNIT-5: D-BLOCK ELEMENTS

Oxidation states and their stability; standard electrode potentials; interstitial compounds; alloys; catalytic properties; applications; preparation, structure, and reactions of oxoanions of chromium and manganese.

UNIT-6: F BLOCK ELEMENTS

Lanthanoid and actinoid contractions; oxidation states; general characteristics.

UNIT-7: COORDINATION COMPOUNDS

Werner's theory; Nomenclature, cis-trans and ionization isomerism, hybridization and geometries (linear, tetrahedral, square planar and octahedral) of mononuclear coordination compounds; Bonding [VBT and CFT (octahedral and tetrahedral fields)]; Magnetic properties (spin-only) and colour of 3d-series coordination compounds; Ligands and spectrochemical series; Stability; Importance and applications; Metal carbonyls.

UNIT-8:Isolation of Metals

Metal ores and their concentration; extraction of crude metal from concentrated ores: thermodynamic (iron, copper, zinc) and electrochemical (aluminium) principles of metallurgy; cyanide process (silver and gold); refining.

UNIT-9: Principles of Qualitative Analysis

Groups I to V (only Ag^+, Hg_2^+, Cu^{2+}, Pb^{2+}, Fe^{3+}, Cr^{3+}, Al^{3+}, Ca^{2+}, Ba^{2+}, Zn^{2+}, Mn^{2+} and Mg^{2+});
Nitrate, halides (excluding fluoride), carbonate and bicarbonate, sulphate and sulphide.

UNIT-10: Environmental Chemistry

Atmospheric pollution; water pollution; soil pollution; industrial waste; strategies to control
environmental pollution; green chemistry.

ORGANIC CHEMSITRY

UNIT-1:Basic Principles of Organic Chemistry

Hybridisation of carbon; σ and π-bonds; Shapes of simple organic molecules; aromaticity;
(R,S and E,Z configurations excluded); Determination of empirical and molecular formulae of
simple compounds by combustion method only; IUPAC nomenclature of organic molecules
(hydrocarbons, including simple cyclic hydrocarbons and their mono-functional and bi-functional
derivatives only); Hydrogen bonding effects; Inductive, Resonance and Hyperconjugative effects;
Acidity and basicity of organic compounds; Reactive intermediates produced during homolytic
and heterolytic bond cleavage; Formation, structure and stability of carbocations, carbanions and
free radicals.

UNIT-2: Alkanes

Homologous series; Physical properties (melting points, boiling points and density) and effect of
branching on them; Conformations of ethane and butane (Newman projections only); Preparation
from alkyl halides and aliphatic carboxylic acids; Reactions: combustion, halogenation (including
allylic and benzylic halogenation) and oxidation.

UNIT-3:Alkenes and Alkynes

Physical properties (boiling points, density and dipole moments); Preparation by elimination
reactions; Acid catalysed hydration (excluding the stereochemistry of addition and elimination);
Metal acetylides; Reactions of alkenes with $KMnO4$ and ozone; Reduction of alkenes and alkynes;
Electrophilic addition reactions of alkenes with X_2, HX, HOX, (X=halogen); Effect of peroxide
on addition reactions; cyclic polymerization reaction of alkynes.

UNIT-4: Benzene

Structure; Electrophilic substitution reactions: halogenation, nitration, sulphonation, Friedel-
Crafts alkylation and acylation; Effect of directing groups (monosubstituted benzene) in these
reactions.

UNIT-5:Phenols

Physical properties; Preparation, Electrophilic substitution reactions of phenol (halogenation,
nitration, sulphonation); Reimer-Tiemann reaction, Kolbe reaction; Esterification; Etherification;
Aspirin synthesis; Oxidation and reduction reactions of phenol.

UNIT-6:Alkyl Halides

Rearrangement reactions of alkyl carbocation; Grignard reactions; Nucleophilic substitution
reactions and their stereochemical aspects.

UNIT-7:Alcohols

Physical properties; Reactions: esterification, dehydration (formation of alkenes and ethers);
Reactions with: sodium, phosphorus halides, $ZnCl2$/concentrated HCl, thionyl chloride;
Conversion of alcohols into aldehydes, ketones and carboxylic acids.

UNIT-8:Ethers
Preparation by Williamson's synthesis; C-O bond cleavage reactions.

UNIT-9:Aldehydes and Ketones
Preparation of: aldehydes and ketones from acid chlorides and nitriles; aldehydes from esters; benzaldehyde from toluene and benzene; Reactions: oxidation, reduction, oxime and hydrazone formation; Aldol condensation, Cannizzaro reaction; Haloform reaction; Nucleophilic addition reaction with RMgX, NaHSO3, HCN, alcohol, amine.

UNIT-10:Carboxylic Acids
Physical properties; Preparation: from nitriles, Grignard reagents, hydrolysis of esters and amides; Preparation of benzoic acid from alkylbenzenes; Reactions: reduction, halogenation, formation of esters, acid chlorides and amides.

UNIT-11:Amines
Preparation from nitro compounds, nitriles and amides; Reactions: Hoffmann bromamide degradation, Gabriel phthalimide synthesis; Reaction with nitrous acid, Azo coupling reaction of diazonium salts of aromatic amines; Sandmeyer and related reactions of diazonium salts; Carbylamine reaction, Hinsberg test, Alkylation and acylation reactions.

UNIT-12:Haloarenes
Reactions: Fittig, Wurtz-Fittig; Nucleophilic aromatic substitution in haloarenes and substituted haloarenes (excluding benzyne mechanism and cine substitution).

UNIT-13:Biomolecules
Carbohydrates: Classification; Mono- and di-saccharides (glucose and sucrose); Oxidation; Reduction; Glycoside formation and hydrolysis of disaccharides (sucrose, maltose, lactose);

UNIT-14:NANOMERS
Proteins: Amino acids; Peptide linkage; Structure of peptides (primary and secondary); Types of proteins (fibrous and globular).
Nucleic acids: Chemical composition and structure of DNA and RNA.

UNIT-17:Polymers
Types of polymerization (addition, condensation); Homo and copolymers; Natural rubber; Cellulose; Nylon; Teflon; Bakelite; PVC; Bio-degradable polymers; Applications of polymers.

UNIT-18:Chemistry in Everyday Life
Drug-target interaction; Therapeutic action, and examples (excluding structures), of antacids, antihistamines, tranquilizers, analgesics, antimicrobials, and antifertility drugs; Artificial sweeteners (names only); Soaps, detergents, and cleansing action.

UNIT-18:PRACTICAL ORGANIC CHEMISTRY
Detection of elements (N, S, halogens); Detection and identification of the following functional groups: hydroxyl (alcoholic and phenolic), carbonyl (aldehyde and ketone), carboxyl, amino and nitro.

3.2.1.3:MATHEMATICS:

UNIT-1: SETS,RELATIONS,FUNCTIONS:

Sets and their representations, different kinds of sets (empty, finite and infinite), algebra of sets, intersection, complement, difference and symmetric difference of sets and their algebraic properties, De-Morgan's laws on union, intersection, difference (for finite number of sets) and practical problems based on them.

Cartesian product of finite sets, ordered pair, relations, domain and codomain of relations, equivalence relation

Function as a special case of relation, functions as mappings, domain, codomain, range of functions, invertible functions, even and odd functions, into, onto and one-to-one functions, special functions (polynomial, trigonometric, exponential, logarithmic, power, absolute value, greatest integer etc.), sum, difference, product and composition of functions.

UNIT-2: ALGEBRA

Algebra of complex numbers, addition, multiplication, conjugation, polar representation, properties of modulus and principal argument, triangle inequality, cube roots of unity, geometric interpretations.

Statement of fundamental theorem of algebra, Quadratic equations with real coefficients, relations between roots and coefficients, formation of quadratic equations with given roots, symmetric functions of roots.

Arithmetic and geometric progressions, arithmetic and geometric means, sums of finite arithmetic and geometric progressions, infinite geometric series, sum of the first n natural numbers, sums of squares and cubes of the first n natural numbers.

Logarithms and their properties, permutations and combinations, binomial theorem for a positive integral index, properties of binomial coefficients.

Matrices

Matrices as a rectangular array of real numbers, equality of matrices, addition, multiplication by a scalar and product of matrices, transpose of a matrix, elementary row and column transformations, determinant of a square matrix of order up to three, adjoint of a matrix, inverse of a square matrix of order up to three, properties of these matrix operations, diagonal, symmetric and skew-symmetric matrices and their properties, solutions of simultaneous linear equations in two or three variables.

UNIT-3: PROBABILITY & STATISTICS

Random experiment, sample space, different types of events (impossible, simple, compound), addition and multiplication rules of probability, conditional probability, independence of events, total probability, Bayes Theorem, computation of probability of events using permutations and combinations.

Measure of central tendency and dispersion, mean, median, mode, mean deviation, standard deviation and variance of grouped and ungrouped data, analysis of the frequency distribution with same mean but different variance, random variable, mean and variance of the random variable.

UNIT-4: TRIGNOMETRY

Trigonometric functions, their periodicity and graphs, addition and subtraction formulae, formulae involving multiple and sub-multiple angles, general solution of trigonometric equations.

Inverse trigonometric functions (principal value only) and their elementary properties.

UNIT-5: ANALYTICAL GEOMETRY

Two dimensions: Cartesian coordinates, distance between two points, section formulae, shift of origin.

Equation of a straight line in various forms, angle between two lines, distance of a point from a line; Lines through the point of intersection of two given lines, equation of the bisector of the angle between two lines, concurrency of lines; Centroid, orthocentre, incentre and circumcentre of a triangle.

Equation of a circle in various forms, equations of tangent, normal and chord. Parametric equations of a circle, intersection of a circle with a straight line or a circle, equation of a circle through the points of intersection of two circles and those of a circle and a straight line.

Equations of a parabola, ellipse and hyperbola in standard form, their foci, directrices and eccentricity, parametric equations, equations of tangent and normal.

Locus problems.

Three dimensions: Distance between two points, direction cosines and direction ratios, equation of a straight line in space, skew lines, shortest distance between two lines, equation of a plane, distance of a point from a plane, angle between two lines, angle between two planes, angle between a line and the plane, coplanar lines.

Differential Calculus

Limit of a function at a real number, continuity of a function, limit and continuity of the sum, difference, product and quotient of two functions, L'Hospital rule of evaluation of limits of functions.

Continuity of composite functions, intermediate value property of continuous functions.

Derivative of a function, derivative of the sum, difference, product and quotient of two functions, chain rule, derivatives of polynomial, rational, trigonometric, inverse trigonometric, exponential and logarithmic functions.

Tangents and normals, increasing and decreasing functions, derivatives of order two, maximum and minimum values of a function, Rolle's theorem and Lagrange's mean value theorem, geometric interpretation of the two theorems, derivatives up to order two of implicit functions, geometric interpretation of derivatives.

Integral Calculus

Integration as the inverse process of differentiation, indefinite integrals of standard functions, definite integrals as the limit of sums, definite integral and their properties, fundamental theorem of integral calculus.

Integration by parts, integration by the methods of substitution and partial fractions, application of definite integrals to the determination of areas bounded by simple curves. Formation of ordinary

differential equations, solution of homogeneous differential equations of first order and first degree, separation of variables method, linear first order differential equations.

9Vectors

Addition of vectors, scalar multiplication, dot and cross products, scalar and vector triple products, and their geometrical interpretations.

3.2.2:JEE Main Syllabus:

FIG-37:DETAILED SYLLABUS FOR JEE MAIN

3.2.2.1:Physics:

Below is the list of important chapters of Physics. Candidates should cover the entire JEE Main syllabus 2022 of Physics to score good marks. Click Here to download the JEE Mains syllabus PDF of Physics

Section A

Physics and measurement,Rotational motion,Thermodynamics,Kinematics,Work, energy and power,Properties of solids and liquids,Gravitation,Laws of motion,Oscillations and waves,Electronic devices,Kinetic theory of gases,Current electricity,Communication systems,Electromagnetic induction and alternating currents,Magnetic effects of current and magnetism,Optics,Electromagnetic waves,Atoms and nuclei,Electrostatics,Dual nature of matter and radiation

Section B

Experimental Skills

3.2.2.2:CHEMISTRY:

Chemistry is further divided into Physical, Organic and Inorganic chemistry.

1.Physical Chemistry:

Some basic concepts in chemistry,States of matter,Atomic structure,Chemical bonding and molecular structure,Chemical thermodynamics,Solutions,Equilibrium,Redox reactions and electrochemistryChemical kinetics,Surface chemistry

2.Organic Chemistry:

Purification and characterisation of organic compounds,Hydrocarbons,Chemistry in everyday life,Principles related to practical chemistry,Organic compounds containing halogens,Organic compounds containing oxygen,Organic compounds containing nitrogen Polymers,Some basic principles of organic chemistry,Biomolecules

3.Inorganic Chemistry:

Classification of elements and periodicity in properties,Hydrogen,Block elements (alkali and alkaline earth metals),P Block elements group 13 to group 18 elements,d- and f - block elements,Co-ordination compounds,Environmental chemistry,General principles and processes of isolation of metals

3.2.2.3:Mathematics :

Complex numbers and quadratic equations,Matrices and determinants,Sets, relations and functions
Mathematical induction,Permutations and combinations,Mathematical reasoning
Limit, continuity and differentiability,Integral calculus,Three-dimensional geometry
Differential equations,Binomial theorem and its simple applications,Sequence and Series,Vector algebra
Statistics and probability,Trigonometry,Co-ordinate geometry

3.2.3: DETAILED SYLLABUS FOR ICAR:

FIG-38:DETAILED SYLLABUS FOR ICAR

PHYSICS:
Unit-1: Physical World and Measurement
Physics scope and excitement; nature of physical laws; Physics, technology and society. Need for measurement: Units of measurement; systems of units; SI units, fundamental and derived units. Length, mass and time measurements; accuracy and precision of measuring instruments; errors in measurement; significant figures. Dimensions of physical quantities, dimensional analysis and its applications.
Unit-2: Kinematics
Frame of reference. Motion in a straight line: Position-time graph, speed and velocity. Uniform and non-uniform motion, average speed and instantaneous velocity. Uniformly accelerated motion: velocity-time graph, position-time graphs, relations for uniformly accelerated motion (graphical treatment). Elementary concepts of differentiation and integration for describing motion. Scalar and vector quantities: Position and displacement vectors, general vectors and notation, equality of vectors, multiplication of vectors by a real number; addition and subtraction of vectors. Relative velocity. Unit vector; Resolution of a vector in a plane - rectangular components. Motion in a plane. Cases of uniform velocity and uniform acceleration-projectile motion. Uniform circular motion. Motion of objects in three dimensional space. Motion of objects in three dimensional space.

Unit-3: Laws of Motion

Intuitive concept of force. Inertia, Newton's first law of motion; momentum and Newton's second law of motion; impulse; Newton's third law of motion. Law of conservation of linear momentum and its applications. Equilibrium of concurrent forces. Static and kinetic friction, laws of friction, rolling friction. Dynamics of uniform circular motion: Centripetal force, examples of circular motion (vehicle on level circular road, vehicle on banked road).

Unit-4: Work, Energy and Power

Scalar product of vectors. Work done by a constant force and a variable force; kinetic energy, work-energy theorem, power. Notion of potential energy, potential energy of a spring, conservative forces: conservation of mechanical energy (kinetic and potential energies); non-conservative forces: elastic and inelastic collisions in one and two dimensions.

Unit-5: Motion of System of Particles and Rigid Body

Centre of mass of a two-particle system, momentum conversation and centre of mass motion. Centre of mass of a rigid body; centre of mass of uniform rod. Vector product of vectors; moment of a force, torque, angular momentum, conservation of angular momentum with some examples. Equilibrium of rigid bodies, rigid body rotation and equations of rotational motion, comparison of linear and rotational motions; moment of inertia, radius of gyration. Values of moments of inertia for simple geometrical objects. Statement of parallel and perpendicular axes theorems and their applications.

Unit-6: Gravitation

Keplar's laws of planetary motion. The universal law of gravitation. Acceleration due to gravity and its variation with altitude and depth. Gravitational potential energy; gravitational potential. Escape velocity. Orbital velocity of a satellite. Geo-stationary satellites.

Unit-7: Properties of Bulk Matter

Elastic behaviour, Stress-strain relationship, Hooke's law, Young's modulus, bulk modulus, shear, modulus of rigidity. Pressure due to a fluid column; Pascal's law and its applications (hydraulic lift and hydraulic brakes). Effect of gravity on fluid pressure. Viscosity, Stokes' law, terminal velocity, Reynold's number, streamline and turbulent flow. Bernoulli's theorem and its applications. Surface energy and surface tension, angle of contact, application of surface tension ideas to drops, bubbles and capillary rise.

Heat, temperature, thermal expansion; specific heat - calorimetry; change of state - latent heat. Heat transfer- conduction, convection and radiation, thermal conductivity, Newton's law of cooling.

Unit-8: Thermodynamics

Thermal equilibrium and definition of temperature (zeroth law of thermodynamics). Heat, work and internal energy. First law of thermodynamics. Second law of thermodynamics: reversible and irreversible processes. Heat engines and refrigerators.

Unit-9: Behaviour of Perfect Gas and Kinetic Theory

Equation of state of a perfect gas, work done on compressing a gas. Kinetic theory of gases - assumptions, concept of pressure. Kinetic energy and temperature; rms speed of gas molecules; degrees of freedom, law of equipartition of energy (statement only) and application to specific heats of gases; concept of mean free path, Avogadro's number.

Unit-10: Oscillations and Waves

Periodic motion - period, frequency, displacement as a function of time. Periodic functions. Simple Harmonic Motion (S.H.M) and its equation; phase; oscillations of a spring–restoring force and force constant; energy in S.H.M.- kinetic and potential energies; simple pendulum– derivation of expression for its time period; free, forced and damped oscillations, resonance. Wave motion. Longitudinal and transverse waves, speed of wave motion. Displacement relation for a progressive wave. Principle of superposition of waves, reflection of waves, standing waves in strings and organ pipes, fundamental mode and harmonics, Beats, Doppler effect.

Unit-11: Electrostatics

Electric Charges; Conservation of charge, Coulomb's law - force between two point charges, forces between multiple charges; superposition principle and continuous charge distribution. Electric field, electric field due to a point charge, electric field lines; electric dipole, electric field due to a dipole; torque on a dipole in uniform electric field. Electric flux, statement of Gauss's theorem and its applications to find field due to infinitely long straight wire, uniformly charged infinite plane sheet and uniformly charged thin spherical shell (field inside and outside). Electric potential, potential difference, electric potential due to a point charge, a dipole and system of charges; equipotential surfaces, electrical potential energy of a system of two point charges and of electric dipole in an electrostatic field. Conductors and insulators, free charges and bound charges inside a conductor. Dielectrics and electric polarization, capacitors and capacitance, combination of capacitors in series and in parallel, capacitance of a parallel plate capacitor with and without dielectric medium between the plates, energy stored in a capacitor. Van de Graaff generator.

Unit-12: Current Electricity

Electric current, flow of electric charges in a metallic conductor, drift velocity, mobility and their relation with electric current; Ohm's law, electrical resistance, V - I characteristics (linear and non-linear), electrical energy and power, electrical resistivity and conductivity. Carbon resistors, colour code for carbon resistors; series and parallel combinations of resistors; temperature dependence of resistance. Internal resistance of a cell, potential difference and emf of a cell, combination of cells in series and in parallel. Kirchoff's laws and simple applications. Wheatstone bridge, metre bridge. Potentiometer - principle and its applications to measure potential difference and for comparing emf of two cells; measurement of internal resistance of a cell.

Unit-13: Magnetic Effects of Current and Magnetism

Concept of magnetic field, Oersted's experiment. Biot - Savart law and its application to current carrying circular loop. Ampere's law and its applications to infinitely long straight wire, straight and toroidal solenoids. Force on a moving charge in uniform magnetic and electric fields. Cyclotron. Force on a current-carrying conductor in a uniform magnetic field. Force between two parallel current-carrying conductors-definition of ampere. Torque experienced by a current loop in uniform magnetic field; moving coil galvanometer-its current sensitivity and conversion to ammeter and voltmeter.

Current loop as a magnetic dipole and its magnetic dipole moment. Magnetic dipole moment of a revolving electron. Magnetic field intensity due to a magnetic dipole (bar magnet) along its axis and perpendicular to its axis. Torque on a magnetic dipole (bar magnet) in a uniform magnetic field; bar magnet as an equivalent solenoid, magnetic field lines; Earth's magnetic field and magnetic elements. Para-, dia- and ferro - magnetic substances, with examples. Electromagnets and factors affecting their strengths. Permanent magnets.

Unit-14: Electromagnetic Induction and Alternating Currents

Electromagnetic induction; Faraday's law, induced emf and current; Lenz's Law, Eddy currents. Self and mutual inductance. Need for displacement current. Alternating currents, peak and rms value of alternating current/voltage; reactance and impedance; LC oscillations (qualitative treatment only), LCR series circuit, resonance; power in AC circuits, wattless current. AC generator and transformer.

Unit-15: Electromagnetic waves

Displacement current, Electromagnetic waves and their characteristics (qualitative ideas only). Transverse nature of electromagnetic waves. Electromagnetic spectrum (radio waves, microwaves, infrared, visible, ultraviolet, X-rays, gamma rays) including elementary facts about their uses.

Unit-16: Optics

Reflection of light, spherical mirrors, mirror formula. Refraction of light, total internal reflection and its applications, optical fibres, refraction at spherical surfaces, lenses, thin lens formula, lensmaker's formula. Magnification, power of a lens, combination of thin lenses in contact. Refraction and dispersion of light through a prism. Scattering of light - blue colour of the sky and reddish appearance of the sun at sunrise and sunset. Optical instruments: Human eye, image formation and accommodation, correction of eye defects (myopia, hypermetropia, presbyopia and astigmatism) using lenses. Microscopes and astronomical telescopes (reflecting and refracting) and their magnifying powers. Wave optics: wave front and Huygens' principle, reflection and refraction of plane wave at a plane surface using wave fronts. Proof of laws of reflection and refraction using Huygens' principle. Interference, Young's double slit experiment and expression for fringe width, coherent sources and sustained interference of light. Diffraction due to a single slit, width of central maximum. Resolving power of microscopes and astronomical telescopes. Polarisation, plane polarised light; Brewster's law, uses of plane polarised light and Polaroids.

Unit-17: Dual Nature of Matter and Radiation

Dual nature of radiation. Photoelectric effect, Hertz and Lenard's observations; Einstein's photoelectric equation-particle nature of light. Matter waves-wave nature of particles, de Broglie relation. Davisson-Germer experiment.

Unit-18: Atoms & Nuclei

Alpha-particle scattering experiment; Rutherford's model of atom; Bohr model, energy levels, hydrogen spectrum. Composition and size of nucleus, atomic masses, isotopes, isobars; isotones. Radioactivity, alpha, beta and gamma particles/rays and their properties; radioactive decay law. Mass-energy relation, mass defect; binding energy per nucleon and its variation with mass number; nuclear fission, nuclear reactor, nuclear fusion.

Unit-19: Electronic Devices

Semiconductors; semiconductor diode – I -V characteristics in forward and reverse bias, diode as a rectifier; I - V characteristics of LED, photodiode, solar cell, and Zener diode; Zener diode as a voltage regulator. Junction transistor, transistor action, characteristics of a transistor; transistor as an amplifier (common emitter configuration) and oscillator. Logic gates (OR, AND, NOT, NAND and NOR). Transistor as a switch.

Unit-20: Communication Systems

Elements of a communication system (block diagram only); bandwidth of signals (speech, TV and digital data); bandwidth of transmission medium. Propagation of electromagnetic waves in the atmosphere, sky and space wave propagation. Need for modulation. Production and detection of an amplitude-modulated wave.

CHEMISTRY:

Unit-1: Some Basic Concepts of Chemistry

General Introduction: Importance and scope of chemistry. Historical approach to particulate nature of matter, laws of chemical combination. Dalton's atomic theory: concept of elements, atoms and molecules. Atomic and molecular masses mole concept and molar mass: percentage composition, empirical and molecular formula chemical reactions, stoichiometry and calculations based on stoichiometry.

Unit-2: Solid State

Classification of solids based on different binding forces: molecular, ionic, covalent and metallic solids, amorphous and crystalline solids (elementary idea), unit cell in two dimensional and three dimensional lattices, calculation of density of unit cell, packing in solids, voids, number of atoms per unit cell in a cubic unit cell, point defects, electrical and magnetic properties.

Unit-3: Solutions

Types of solutions, expression of concentration of solutions of solids in liquids, solubility of gases in liquids, solid solutions, colligative properties – relative lowering of vapour pressure, elevation of Boiling Point, depression of freezing point, osmotic pressure, determination of molecular masses using colligative properties, abnormal molecular mass.

Unit-4: Structure of Atom

Discovery of electron, proton and neutron; atomic number, isotopes and isobars. Thomson's model and its limitations, Rutherford's model and its limitations. Bohr's model and its limitations, concept of shells and subshells, dual nature of matter and light, de Broglie's relationship, Heisenberg uncertainty principle, concept of orbitals, quantum numbers, shapes of s, p, and d orbitals, rules for filling electrons in orbitals - Aufbau principle, Pauli exclusion principle and Hund's rule, electronic configuration of atoms, stability of half filled and completely filled orbitals.

Unit-5: Classification of Elements and Periodicity in Properties

Significance of classification, brief history of the development of periodic table, modern periodic law and the present form of periodic table, periodic trends in properties of elements -atomic radii, ionic radii. Ionization enthalpy, electron gain enthalpy, electro negativity, valence.

Unit-6: Chemical Bonding and Molecular Structure

Valence electrons, ionic bond, covalent bond: bond parameters. Lewis structure, polar character of covalent bond, covalent character of ionic bond, valence bond theory, resonance, geometry of covalent molecules, VSEPR (Valence shell electron pair repulsion) theory, concept of hybridization, involving s, p and d orbitals and shapes of some simple molecules, molecular orbital; theory of homonuclear diatomic molecules (qualitative idea only), hydrogen bond.

Unit-7: States of Matter: Gases and Liquids

Three states of matter. Intermolecular interactions, type of bonding, melting and boiling points. Role of gas laws in elucidating the concept of the molecule, Boyle's law. Charles law, Gay Lussac's law, Avogadro's law. Ideal behaviour, empirical derivation of gas equation, Avogadro's number. Ideal gas equation. Derivation from ideal behaviour, liquefaction of gases, critical temperature. Liquid State - Vapour pressure, viscosity and surface tension (qualitative idea only, no mathematical derivations).

Unit-8: Thermodynamics

Concepts of System, types of systems, surroundings. Work, heat, energy, extensive and intensive properties, state functions. First law of thermodynamics - internal energy and enthalpy, heat capacity and specific heat, measurement of DU and DH, Hess's law of constant heat summation, enthalpy of: bond dissociation, combustion, formation, atomization, sublimation. Phase transformation, ionization, and solution. Introduction of entropy as a state function, free energy change for spontaneous and non-spontaneous processes, criteria for equilibrium.

Unit-9: Equilibrium

Equilibrium in physical and chemical processes, dynamic nature of equilibrium, law of mass action, equilibrium constant, factors affecting equilibrium - Le Chatelier's principle; ionic equilibrium - ionization of acids and bases, strong and weak electrolytes, degree of ionization, concept of pH. Hydrolysis of salts. Buffer solutions, solubility product, common ion effect.

Unit-10: Redox Reactions

Concept of oxidation and reduction, redox reactions, oxidation number, balancing redox reactions, applications of redox reactions.

Unit-11: Hydrogen

Position of hydrogen in periodic table, occurrence, isotopes, preparation, properties and uses of hydrogen; hydrides - ionic, covalent and interstitial; physical and chemical properties of water, heavy water; hydrogen peroxide-preparation, properties and structure; hydrogen as a fuel.

Unit-12: s-Block Elements (Alkali and Alkaline earth metals)

Group 1 and Group 2 elements

General introduction, electronic configuration, occurrence, anomalous properties of the first element of each group, diagonal relationship, trends in the variation of properties (such as ionization enthalpy, atomic and ionic radii), trends in chemical reactivity with oxygen, water, hydrogen and halogens; uses.

Unit-13: Preparation and properties of some important compounds

Sodium carbonate, sodium chloride, sodium hydroxide and sodium hydrogen carbonate, biological importance of sodium and potassium. CaO, CaCO3 and industrial use of lime and limestone, biological importance of Mg and Ca

Unit-14: Some p-Block Elements

General Introduction to p-Block Elements: Group 13 elements

General introduction, electronic configuration, occurrence. Variation of properties, oxidation states, trends in chemical reactivity, anomalous properties of first element of the group; Boron- physical and chemical properties, some important compounds: borax, boric acids, boron hydrides. Aluminum: uses, reactions with acids and alkalies.

Unit-15: Group 14 elements

General introduction, electronic configuration, occurrence, variation of properties, oxidation states, trends in chemical reactivity, anomalous behavior of first element, Carbon - catenation, allotropic forms, physical and chemical properties; uses of some important compounds: oxides. Important compounds of silicon and a few uses: silicon tetrachloride, silicones, silicates and zeolites.

Unit-16: Organic Chemistry

Some Basic Principles and Techniques

General introduction, methods of qualitative and quantitative analysis, classification and IUPAC nomenclature of organic compounds, Electronic displacements in a covalent bond: inductive effect, electromeric effect, resonance and hyper conjugation. Homolytic and heterolytic fission of a covalent bond: free radicals, carbocations, carbanions; electrophiles and nucleophiles, types of organic reactions

Unit-17: Hydrocarbons

Classification of hydrocarbons

Alkanes - Nomenclature, isomerism, conformations (ethane only), physical properties, chemical reactions including free radical mechanism of halogenation, combustion and pyrolysis.

Alkenes - Nomenclature, structure of double bond (ethene) geometrical isomerism, physical properties, methods of preparation; chemical reactions: addition of hydrogen, halogen, water, hydrogen halides (Markovnikov's addition and peroxide effect), ozonolysis, oxidation, mechanism of electrophilic addition.

Alkynes - Nomenclature, structure of triple bond (ethyne), physical properties. Methods of preparation, chemical reactions: acidic character of alkynes, addition reaction of - hydrogen, halogens, hydrogen halides and water.

Aromatic hydrocarbons: Introduction, IUPAC nomenclature; benzene: resonance, aromaticity; chemical properties: mechanism of electrophilic substitution. – nitration, sulphonation, halogenation, Friedel-Craft's alkylation and acylation: directive influence of functional group in mono-substituted benzene; carcinogenicity and toxicity.

Unit-18: Electrochemistry

Conductance in electrolytic solutions, specific and molar conductivity variations of conductivity with concentration, Kohlrausch's Law, electrolysis and laws of electrolysis (elementary idea), dry cell – electrolytic cells and Galvanic cells; lead accumulator, EMF of a cell, standard electrode potential, Nernst equation and its application to chemical cells, fuel cells; corrosion.

Unit-19: Chemical Kinetics

Rate of a reaction (average and instantaneous), factors affecting rate of reaction; concentration, temperature, catalyst; order and molecularity of a reaction; rate law and specific rate constant, integrated rate equations and half life (only for zero and first order reactions); concept of collision theory (elementary idea, no mathematical treatment)

Unit-20: Surface Chemistry

Adsorption – physisorption and chemisorption; factors affecting adsorption of gases on solids; catalysis : homogenous and heterogeneous, activity and selectivity: enzyme catalysis; colloidal state: distinction between true solutions, colloids and suspensions; lyophilic, lyophobic, multimolecular and macromolecular colloids; properties of colloids; Tyndall effect, Brownian movement, electrophoresis, coagulation; emulsion – types of emulsions.

Unit-21: General Principles and Processes of Isolation of Elements

Principles and methods of extraction - concentration, oxidation, reduction electrolytic method and refining; occurrence and principles of extraction of aluminium, copper, zinc and iron.

Unit-22: p-Block Elements

Group 15 elements

General introduction, electronic configuration, occurrence, oxidation states, trends in physical and chemical properties; nitrogen - preparation, properties and uses; compounds of nitrogen: preparation and properties of ammonia and nitric acid, oxides of nitrogen (structure only); Phosphorous-allotropic forms; compounds of phosphorous: preparation and properties of phosphine, halides (PCl_3, PCl_5) and oxoacids

Unit-23: Group 16 elements

General introduction, electronic configuration, oxidation states, occurrence, trends in physical and chemical properties; dioxygen: preparation, properties and uses; simple oxides; Ozone. Sulphur - allotropic forms; compounds of sulphur: preparation, properties and uses of sulphur dioxide; sulphuric acid: industrial process of manufacture, properties and uses, oxoacids of sulphur (structures only).

Unit-24: Group 17 elements

General introduction, electronic configuration, oxidation states, occurrence, trends in physical and chemical properties; compounds of halogens: preparation, properties and uses of chlorine and hydrochloric acid, interhalogen compounds, oxoacids of halogens (structures only).

Unit-25: Group 18 elements

General introduction, electronic configuration. Occurrence, trends in physical and chemical properties, uses.

Unit-26: d and f Block Elements

General introduction ,electronic configuration, occurrence and characteristics of transition metals, general trends in properties of the first row transition metals – metallic character, ionization enthalpy, oxidation states, ionic radii, colour catalytic property, magnetic properties, interstitial compounds, alloy formation preparation and properties of $K_2Cr_2O_7$ and $KMnO_4$.

Lanthanoids - electronic configuration, oxidation states, chemical reactivity and lanthanoid contraction.

Actinoids - Electronic configuration, oxidation states.

Unit-27: Coordination Compounds

Coordination compounds - Introduction, ligands, coordination number, colour, magnetic properties and shapes, IUPAC nomenclature of mononuclear coordination compounds. bonding; isomerism, importance of coordination compounds (in qualitative analysis, extraction of metals and biological systems).

Unit-28: Haloalkanes and Haloarenes

Haloalkanes: Nomenclature, nature of C-X bond, physical and chemical properties, mechanism of substitution reactions.

Haloarenes: Nature of C-X bond, substitution reactions (directive influence of halogen for monosubstituted compounds only) Uses and environmental effects of - dichloromethane, trichloromethane, tetrachloromethane, iodoform, freons, DDT.

Unit-29: Alcohols, Phenols and Ethers

Alcohols

Nomenclature, methods of preparation, physical and chemical properties (of primary alcohols only); identification of primary, secondary and tertiary alcohols; mechanism of dehydration, uses of methanol and ethanol. Phenols : Nomenclature, methods of preparation, physical and chemical properties, acidic nature of phenol, electrophillic substitution reactions, uses of phenols. Ethers: Nomenclature, methods of preparation, physical and chemical properties, uses.

Unit-30: Aldehydes, Ketones and Carboxylic Acids

Aldehydes and Ketones: Nomenclature, nature of carbonyl group, methods of preparation, physical and chemical properties mechanism of nucleophilic addition, reactivity of alpha hydrogen in aldehydes; uses.

Carboxylic Acids: Nomenclature, acidic nature, methods of preparation, physical and chemical properties; uses.

Unit-31: Organic compounds containing Nitrogen

Amines: Nomenclature, classification, structure, methods of preparation, physical and chemical properties, uses, identification of primary, secondary and tertiary amines.

Cyanides and Isocyanides - will be mentioned at relevant places in context.

Diazonium salts: Preparation, chemical reactions and importance in synthetic organic chemistry.

Unit-32: Biomolecules

Carbohydrates- Classification (aldoses and ketoses), monosaccharide (glucose and fructose), oligosaccharides (sucrose, lactose, maltose), polysaccharides (starch, cellulose, glycogen); importance.

Proteins - Elementary idea of á-amino acids, peptide bond, polypeptides, proteins, structure of amines-primary, secondary, tertiary structure and quaternary structures (qualitative idea only), denaturation of proteins; enzymes.

Vitamins - Classification and functions.

Nucleic Acids: DNA and RNA .

Unit-33: Polymers

Classification - natural and synthetic, methods of polymerization (addition and condensation), copolymerization. Some important polymers: natural and synthetic like polythene, nylon, polyesters, Bakelite, rubber.

Unit-34: Environmental Chemistry

Environmental pollution - air, water and soil pollution, chemical reactions in atmosphere, smog, major atmospheric pollutants; acid rain, ozone and its reactions, effects of depletion of ozone layer, greenhouse effect and global warming - pollution due to industrial wastes; green chemistry as an alternative tool for reducing pollution, strategy for control of environmental pollution.

Unit-35: Chemistry in Everyday life

1. Chemicals in medicines - analgesics, tranquilizers, antiseptics, disinfectants, antimicrobials, antifertility drugs, antibiotics, antacids, antihistamines.
2. Chemicals in food - preservatives, artificial sweetening agents.
3. Cleansing agents - soaps and detergents, cleansing action.

BIOLOGY:

BIOLOGY (BOTANY AND ZOOLOGY)

Unit : 1 The Living World

Nature and scope of Biology. Methods of Biology. Our place in the universe. Laws that govern the universe and life. Level of organization. Cause and effect relationship.

Being alive. What does it mean? Present approaches to understand life processes, molecular approach; life as an expression of energy; steady state and homeostasis; self duplication and survival; adaptation; death as a positive part of life.

Origin of life and its maintenance. Origin and diversity of life. Physical and chemical principles that maintain life processes. The living crust and interdependence. The positive and negative aspects of progress in biological sciences. The future of the living world, identification of human responsibility in shaping our future.

Unit : 2 Unit of Life

Cell as a unit of life. Small biomolecules; water, minerals, mono and oligosaccharides, lipids, amino acids, nucleotides and their chemistry, cellular location and function. Macromolecules in cells - their chemistry, cellular location and functional significance. Polysaccharides, proteins and nucleic acids. Enzymes; chemical nature, classification, mechanism in action-enzyme complex, allosteric modulation (brief), irreversible activation. Biomembranes; Fluid mosaic model of membrane, role in transport, recognition of external information (brief). Structural organization of the cell; light and electron microscopic views of cell, its organelles and their functions; nucleus mitochondria, chloroplasts, endoplasmic reticulum. Golgi complex, lysosomes, microtubules, cell wall, cilia and flagella, vacuoles, cell inclusions. A general account of cellular respiration. Fermentation, biological oxidation (A cycle outline), mitochondrial electron transport chain, high energy bonds and oxidative phosphorylation, cell reproduction; Process of mitosis and meiosis.

Unit : 3 Diversity of Life

Introduction. The enormous variety of living things, the need for classification to cope with this variety; taxonomy and phylogeny; shortcomings of a two kingdom classification as plants and animals; the five kingdom classification, Monera, Protista, Plantae, Fungi and Animalia; the basic features of five kingdom classification. modes of obtaining nutrition-autotrophs and heterotrophs. Life style producers, consumers and decomposers. Unicellularity and multicellularity, phylogenetic relationships. Concepts of species, taxon and categories - hierarchical levels of classification; binomial nomenclature; principles of classification and nomenclature; identification and nature of viruses and bacteriophages; kingdom Monera-archeabacteria - life in extreme environments; Bacteria, Actinomycetes, Cyanobacteria. Examples & illustration of autotrophic and heterotrophic life; mineralizes-nitrogen fixers; Monera in cycling matter; symbiotic forms; disease producers. Kingdom Protista-Eukaryotic unicellular organisms, development of flagella and cilia; beginning of mitosis; syngamy and sex. Various life styles shown in the major phyla. Evolutionary precursors of complex life forms. Diatoms, dinoflagellates, slime moulds, protozons; symbiotic forms. Plant kingdom-complex autotrophs, red brown and green algae; conquest of land, bryophytes, ferns, gymnosperms and angiosperms. Vascularization; development of flower, fruit and seed. Kingdom fungi-lower fungi (Zygomycetes), higher fungi (Ascomycetes and Basidiomycetes); the importance of fungi. Decomposers; parasitic forms; lichens and mycorrhizae. Animal kingdom-animal body pattern and symmetry. The development of body cavity in invertebrate vertebrate physia. Salient features with reference to habitat and example of phylum porifera, coelenterata, helminthis, annelids, mollusca, arthropoda, echinoderms; chordata - (classes-fishes, amphibians, reptiles, birds and mammals) highlighting major characters.

Unit : 4 Organisms and Environment

Species: Origin and concept of species population, interaction between environment and population community. Biotic community, interaction between different species, biotic stability. Changes in the community. Succession. Ecosystem; interaction between biotic and abiotic components; major ecosystems, manmade ecosystem- Agro ecosystem. Biosphere; flow of energy, trapping of solar energy, energy pathway, food chain, food web, biogeochemical cycles, calcium and sulphur, ecological imbalance and its consequences. Conservation of natural resources; renewable and non-renewable (in brief). Water and land management, wasteland development. Wild life and forest conservation; causes for the extinction of some wild life, steps taken to conserve the remaining species, concept of endangered species-Indian examples, conservation of forests; Indian forests, importance of forests, hazards of deforestation, concept of afforestation. Environmental pollution; air and water pollution, sources, major pollutants of big cities of our country, their effects and methods of control, pollution due to nuclear fallout and waste disposal, effect and control, noise pollution; sources and effects.

Unit : 5 Multicellularity : Structure and Function - Plant Life

Form and function. Tissue system in flowering plants; meristematic and permanent. Mineral nutrition-essential elements, major functions of different elements, passive and active uptake of minerals. Modes of nutrition, transport of solutes and water in plants. Photosynthesis; photochemical and biosynthetic phases, diversity in photosynthetic pathways, photosynthetic electron transport and photophosphorylation, photorespiration. Transpiration and exchange of gases. Stomatal mechanism. Osmoregulation in plants: water relations in plant cells, water potential. Reproduction and development in Angiosperms; asexual and sexual reproduction. Structure and functions of flower: development of male and female gametophytes in angiosperms, pollination, fertilization and development of endosperm, embryo seed and fruit. Differentiation and organ formation. Plant hormones and growth regulation; action of plant hormones in relation to seed dormancy and germination, apical dominance, senescence and abscission. Applications of synthetic growth regulators. A brief account of growth and movement in plants.

Unit : 6 Multicellularity : Structure and Function - Animal Life

Animal tissues, epithelial, connective, muscular, nerve. Animal nutrition, organs of digestion and digestive process, nutritional requirements for carbohydrates, proteins, fats, minerals and vitamins; nutritional imbalances and deficiency diseases. Gas exchange and transport: Pulmonary gas exchange and organs involved, transport of gases in blood, gas exchange in aqueous media circulation: closed and open vascular systems , structure and pumping action of heart, arterial blood pressure, lymph. Excretion and osomoregulation. Ammonotelism,

Ureotelism, urecotelism, excretion of water and urea with special reference to man. Role of kidney in regulation of plasma, osmolarity on the basis of nephron structure, skin and lungs in excretion. Hormonal coordination; hormones of mammals, role of hormones as messengers and regulators. Nervous coordination, central autonomic and peripheral nervous systems, receptors, effectors, reflex action, basic physiology of special senses, integrative control by neuroendocrinal systems. Locomotion: joints, muscle movements, types of skeletal muscles according to types of movement, basic aspects of human skeleton. Reproduction; human reproduction, female reproductive cycles. Embryonic development in mammals (upto three germs layers), growth, repair and ageing.

Unit : 7 Continuity of Life

Heredity and variation: Introduction, Mendel's experiments with peas and concepts of factors. Mendel's laws of inheritance. Genes: Packaging of heredity material in prokaryotes-bacterial chromosome and plasmid; and eukaryote chromosomes. Extranuclear genes, viral genes. Linkage (genetic) maps. Sex determination and sex linkage. Genetic material and its replication, gene manipulation. Gene expression; genetic code, transcription, translation, gene regulation. Molecular basis of differentiation.

Unit : 8 Origin and Evolution of Life

Origin of life: living and non-living, chemical evolution, organic evolution; Oparin ideas, Miller-Urey experiments. Interrelationship among living organisms and evidences of evolution: fossil records including geological scale, Morphological evidence - hematology, vestigeal organs, embryological similarities and biogeographical evidence.

Darwin's two major contributions. Common origin of living organisms and recombination as source of variability, selection and variation, adaptation (Lederberg's replica plating experiment for indirect selection of bacterial mutants), reproductive isolation, speciation. Role of selection, change and drift in determining composition of population. Selected examples: industrial melanism; drug resistance, mimicry, malaria in relation to G-6-PD deficiency and sickle cell disease. Human evolution: Palcontological evidence, man's place among mammals. Brief idea of Dryopithecus, Australopithecus, Homo erectus, H.neanderthlensis, Cro-Magnon man and Homo sapiens. Human chromosomes, similarity in different racial groups. Comparison with chromosomes of non-human primates to indicate common origin; Cultural vs. biological evolution.

Mutation: origin and types of mutation, their role in speciation.

Unit : 9 Application of Biology

Introduction, role of biology, in the amelioration of human problems. Domestication of plant- a historical account, improvement of crop plants; Principles of plant breeding and plant introduction. Use of fertilizers, their economic and ecological aspects.

Use of pesticides: advantages and hazards. Biological methods of pest control. Crops today. Current concerns, gene pools and genetic conservation. Underutilized crops with potential uses of oilseeds, medicines, beverages, spices, fodder, New crops-Leucaena (Subabul), Jojoba, Guayule, winged bean, etc. Biofertilizers - green manure, crop residues and nitrogen fixation (symbiotic, non symbiotic). Applications of tissue culture and genetic engineering in crops. Domestication and introduction of animals. Livestock, poultry, fisheries (fresh water, marine, aquaculture). Improvement of animals: principles of animal breeding. Major animal diseases and their control. Insects and their products (silk, honey, wax and lac). Bioenergy-biomass, wood (combustion; gasification, ethanol). Cow dung cakes, gobar gas, plants as sources of hydrocarbons for producing petroleum, ethanol from starch and lignocellulose. Biotechnology, application in health and agriculture, genetically modified (GM) organisms, bio-safety issues. A brief historical account-manufacture of cheese. yoghurt, alcohol, yeast, vitamins, organic acids, antibiotics, steroids, dextrins. Scaling up laboratory findings to Industrial production, sewage treatment. Production of insulin, human growth hormones, interferon. Communicable diseases including STD and diseases spread through 'blood transfusion (hepatitis, AIDS, etc) Immune response, vaccine and antisera. Allergies and Inflammation. Inherited diseases and dysfunctions, sex-linked diseases, genetic incompatibilities, and genetic counseling. Cancer-major types, causes, diagnosis and treatment. Tissue and organ transplantation. Community health services and measures; blood banks; mental health, smoking, alcoholism and drug addiction-physiological symptoms and control measures. Industrial wastes, toxicology, pollution-related diseases. Biomedical engineering - spare parts for man, instruments for diagnosis of diseases and care. Human population related diseases. Human population, growth, problems and control, inequality between sexes, control measures; test-tube babies aminocentesis. Future of Biology.

CHAPTER FOUR

TOPICWISE ANALYSIS

Topicwise analysis is very important for making strategies for better results.

4.1:TOPICWISE ANALYSIS FOR JEE ADVANCED:

Chemistry	
Topic	Weightage
Aldehydes, Ketones and Carboxylic Acids	14-15%
Hydrocarbons	13-14%
P-Block Elements	13-14%
Solid State	4-5%
Atomic Structure	14-15%
Electrochemistry	4-5%
Thermodynamics	6-7%
Organic Chemistry	11-12%
Solutions	6-7%
Coordination Compounds	4-5%
Chemical Bonding	4-5%

FIG-38: TOPICWISE ANALYSIS FOR JEE ADVANCED CHEMISTRY

Chemistry

Topic	Weightage
Electrochemistry	4-5%
Organic Compounds Containing Nitrogen	9-10%
Chemical Kinetics	6-7%
Haloalkanes and Haloarenes	6-7%
Solutions	4-5%
Alcohols, Phenols and Ethers	9-10%
Hydrocarbons	6-7%
Equilibrium in Physical and Chemical Processes	6-7%
Study of First Element: Hydrogen	4-5%
Thermodynamics	4-5%
Some P-Block Elements	6-7%
P-Block Elements	22-23%
Surface Chemistry	6-7%

FIG-39: TOPICWISE ANALYSIS FOR JEE ADVANCED CHEMISTRY

Mathematics

Topic	Weightage
Ellipse	4-5%
Complex Numbers	6-7%
Circles	9-10%
Limits and Continuity	6-7%
Definite Integral	11-12%
Application of Derivatives	14-15%
Hyperbola	6-7%
Sequence and Series	4-5%
Matrices	11-12%
Permutations and Combinations	4-5%
Probability	6-7%
Parabola	11-12%

FIG-40: TOPICWISE ANALYSIS FOR JEE ADVANCED MATHEMATICS

Physics

Topic	Weightage
Alternating Current	6-7%
Current Electricity	6-7%
Kinematics	4-5%
Capacitors	9-10%
Measurement and Errors	4-5%
Rotational Dynamics	29-30%
Electrostatics	6-7%
Magnetism	11-12%
Gravitation	4-5%
Wave Optics	5-6%
Modern Physics	4-5%
Vectors	4-5%

FIG-41: TOPICWISE ANALYSIS FOR JEE ADVANCED PHYSICS

Mathematics	
Topic	Weightage
3D Geometry	20-21%
Probability	4-5%
Theory of Equations	9-10%
Area of Bounded Regions	6-7%
Trigonometry	6-7%
Sets, Relations and Functions	4-5%
Differential Equations	4-5%
Definite Integrals	13-14%
Limits and Continuity	6-7%
Application of Derivatives	19-20%
Matrices	4-5%

FIG-42: TOPICWISE ANALYSIS FOR JEE ADVANCED MATHEMATICS

4.2:TOPICWISE ANALYSIS FOR JEE MAIN:

Chapter	Total Questions	Marks
Modern Physics	5	20
Heat and Thermodynamics	3	12
Optics	3	12
Current Electricity	3	12
Electrostatics	3	12
Magnetics	2	8
Unit, Dimension and Vector	1	4
Kinematics	1	4
Laws of motion	1	4
Work, Power and Energy	1	4
Centre Of Mass, Impulse and Momentum	1	4
Rotation	1	4
Gravitation	1	4

FIG-43: TOPICWISE ANALYSIS FOR JEE MAIN PHYSICS

Simple Harmonic Motion	1	4
Solids and Fluids	1	4
Waves	1	4
Electromagnetics Induction; AC	1	4

FIG-44: TOPICWISE ANALYSIS FOR JEE MAIN PHYSICS

Follow the below-given table for jee mains chapter wise weightage of chemistry.

Chapter No of Questions Marks

Chapter	Total Questions	Marks
Transition Elements and Coordination Chemistry	3	12
Periodic table and Representative Elements	3	12
Thermodynamics And Gaseous State	2	8
Atomic Structure	2	8
Chemical Bonding	2	8
Chemical And Ionic Equilibrium	2	8
Solid-State And Surface Chemistry	2	8

FIG-45: TOPICWISE ANALYSIS FOR JEE MAIN CHEMISTRY

Chapter	Total Questions	Marks
Nuclear Chemistry And Environment	2	8
Mole Concept	1	4
Redox Reaction	1	4
Electrochemistry	1	4
Chemical Kinetics	1	4
Solution and Colligative Properties	1	4
General Organic Chemistry	1	4
Stereochemistry	1	4
Hydrocarbon	1	4
Alkyl Halides	1	4
Carboxylic Acid and their Derivatives	1	4
Carbohydrates, amino acid and Polymers	1	4
Aromatic Compounds	1	4

FIG-46: TOPICWISE ANALYSIS FOR JEE MAIN CHEMISTRY

Chapter	Total Questions	Marks
Coordinate Geometry	5	20
Limits, Continuity and Differentiability	3	12
Integral Calculus	3	12
Complex numbers and Quadratic Equation	2	8
Matrices and Determinants	2	8
Statistics and Probability	2	8
Three Dimensional Geometry	2	8
Vector Algebra	2	8

FIG-47: TOPICWISE ANALYSIS FOR JEE MAIN CHEMISTRY

Sets, Relation and Function	1	4
Permutations and Combinations	1	4
Binomial Theorem and Its Application	1	4
Sequences and Series	1	4
Trigonometry	1	4
Mathematical Reasoning	1	4
Differential Equation	1	4
Statics and Dynamics	1	4
Differential Calculus	1	4

FIG-48: TOPICWISE ANALYSIS FOR JEE MAIN MATHEMATICS

4.3: TOPICWISE ANALYSIS FOR NEET:

NEET Physics Paper Analysis

- Physics section was the toughest and lengthy.
- 4-5 tricky questions were asked in both sections A & B.
- 70% of Physics paper was numerical based.

Topics	Number of Questions
Electrodynamics	20
Mechanics	15
Heat	2
SHM Waves	2
Optics	4
Modern Physics and Electronics	7

FIG-49: TOPICWISE ANALYSIS FOR NEET PHYSICS

NEET Chemistry Paper Analysis

- In comparison to the previous year paper, Chemistry section was difficult.
- Mostly questions were directlty asked from NCERT books.
- Approx 5 questions were matrix match type while 3 questions were graph based.

Topics	Number of Questions
Physical Chemistry	16
Inorganic Chemistry	17
Organic Chemistry	17
Total	50

FIG-50: TOPICWISE ANALYSIS FOR NEET CHEMISTRY

Topics	Number of Questions
Biology in Human Welfare	3
Cell Structure & Functions	9
Diversity of Life	5
Ecology	9
Genetics	11
Plant Physiology	8
Reproduction and Sexual Reproduction	4
Structural organisation of Plants	5
Animal Husbandry & Biotechnology	13
Evolutions	2
Biomolecules	5
Human Health & Disease	2
Human Physiology	10
Human Reproduction & Reproductive Health	6
Structural Ogranisation in Plants	4
Animal Kingdom	4
Total	100

FIG-51: TOPICWISE ANALYSIS FOR NEET BIOLOGY

CHAPTER FIVE

PREVIOUS YEARS QUESTION ANALYSIS

5.1:

Its very necessary to analyze previous years questions of various competitive exams.books are available in the market.

5.2:PREVIOUS YEARS QUESTIONS FOR JEE ADVANCED:

you can refer to the book "JEE ADVANCED SOLVED PAPERS BY ACHARYA VISHVENDRA".
Its available on **amazon.in. flipcart & notion press.**

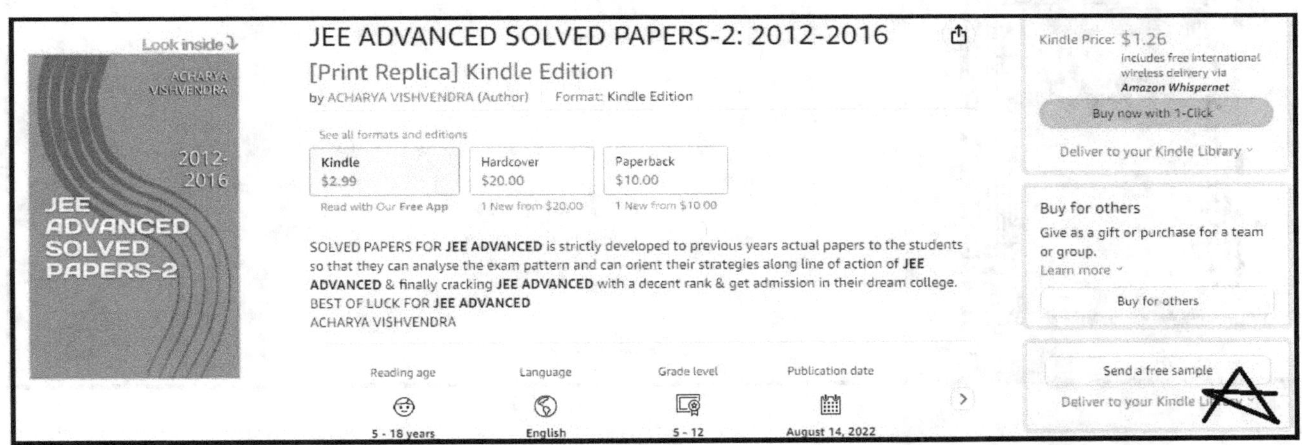

FIG.52: PREVIOUS YEARS QUESTIONS FOR JEE ADVANCED

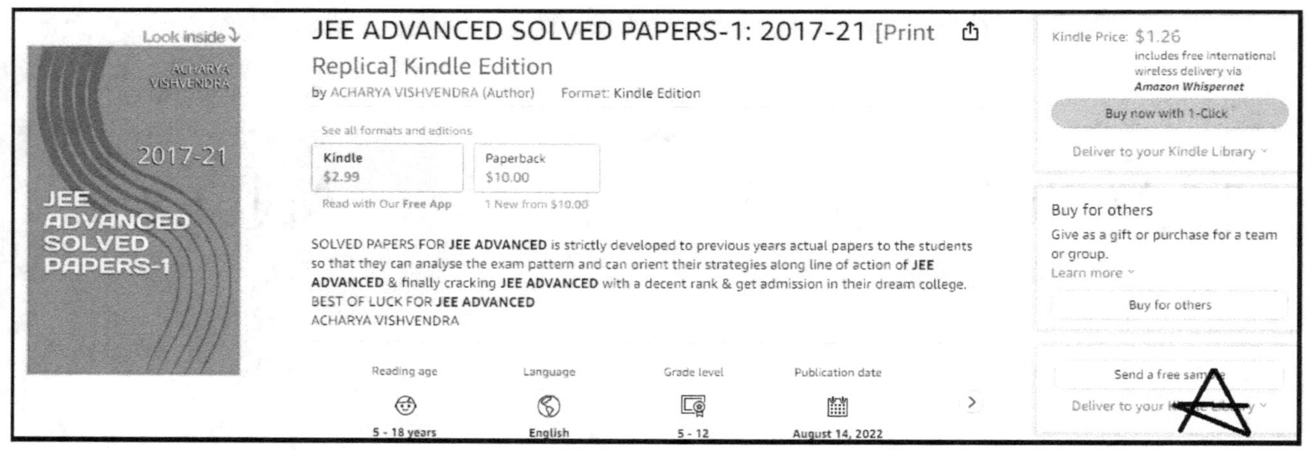

FIG.53: PREVIOUS YEARS QUESTIONS FOR JEE ADVANCED

5.3: PREVIOUS YEARS QUESTIONS FOR JEE MAIN:

FIG.54: PREVIOUS YEARS QUESTIONS FOR JEE ADVANCED

5.4: PREVIOUS YEARS QUESTIONS FOR NTSE:

FIG.55: PREVIOUS YEARS QUESTIONS FOR JEE ADVANCED

5.5: PREVIOUS YEARS QUESTIONS FOR KVPY:

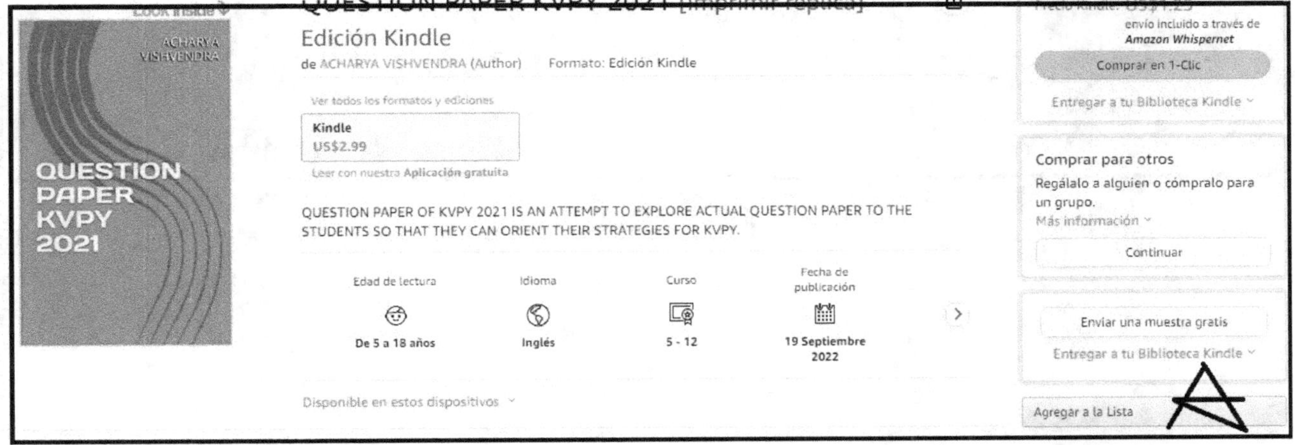

FIG.56: PREVIOUS YEARS QUESTIONS FOR JEE ADVANCED

CHAPTER SIX

DETAILED NOTES

Its very necessary to have detailed notes which are concise & comprehensive so that you have access to each & every information related to competitive exam.

you can also purchase online notes available in the market.you can refer to the book"OPTIMAL PHYSICS FOPR JEE & NEET-1-01 BY ACHARYA VISHVENDRA" for JEE AND NEET.

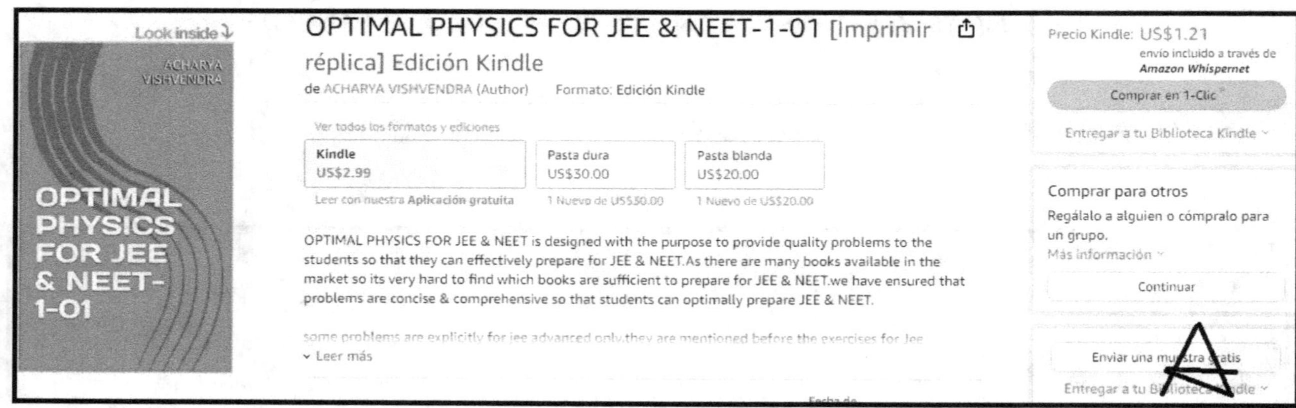

FIG.57: DETAILED NOTES FOR JEE & NEET

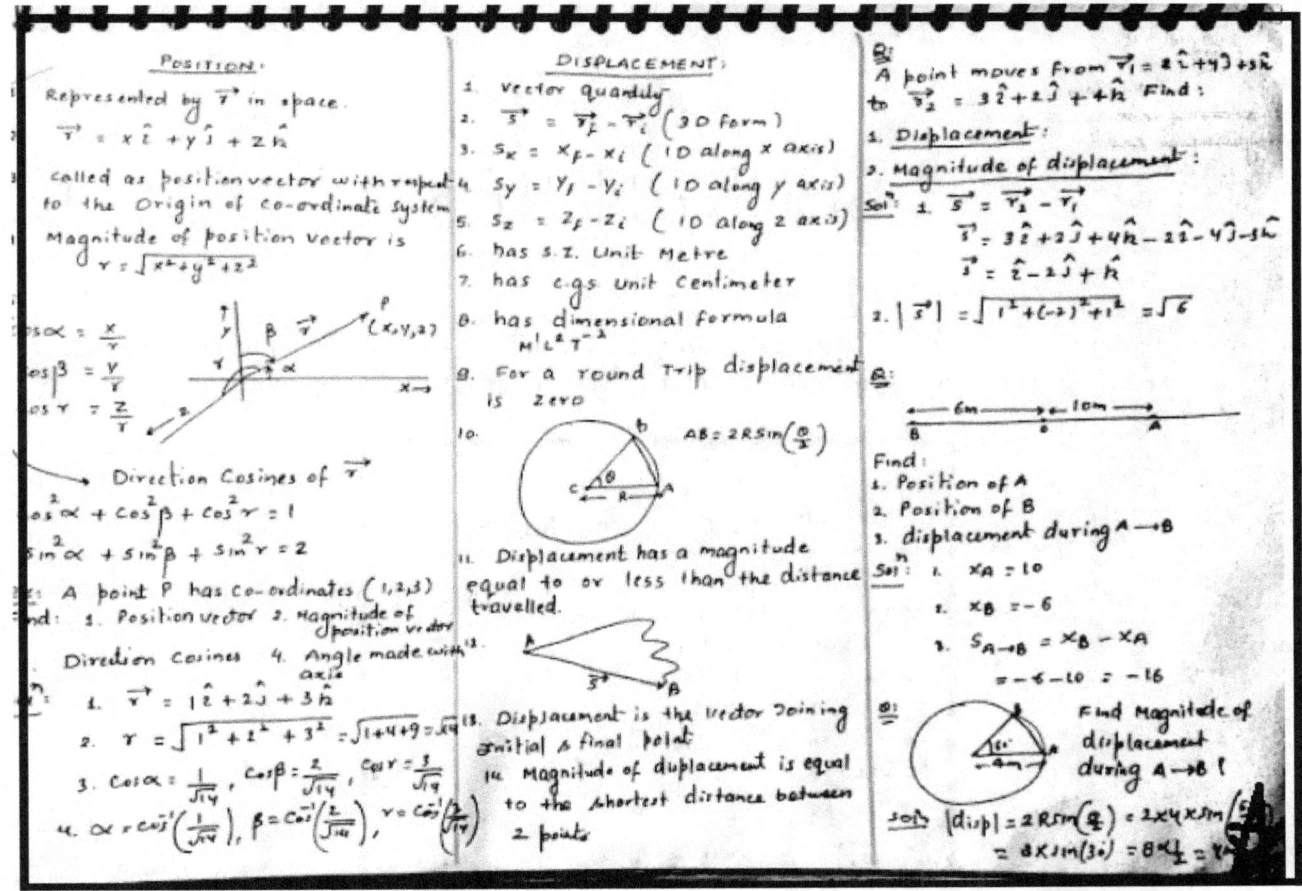

FIG.58: DETAILED NOTES FOR JEE & NEET

CHAPTER SEVEN

SHORT NOTES

After developing short notes its necessary to have short notes which acts as a summary for detailed notes.as its not possible to revise entire detailed notes just before exam so its very necessary to develop short notes.

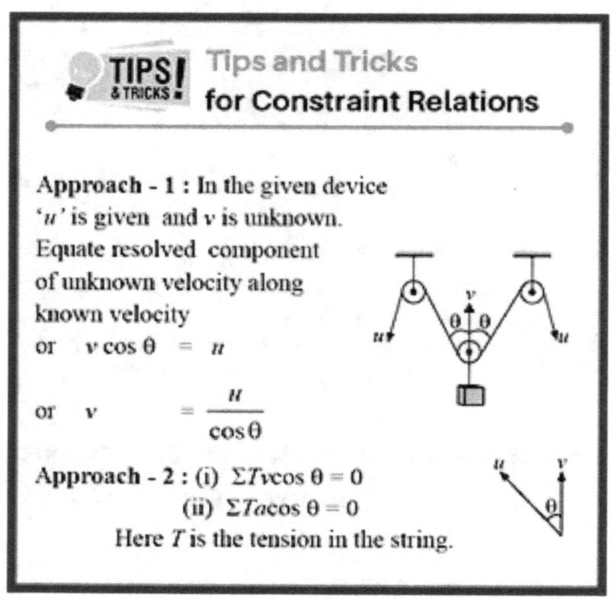

FIG.59: SHORT NOTES FOR JEE PHYSICS

TIPS! & TRICKS

Tips and Tricks for Simple Pulley Devices Shortcut

Generally in pulley devices, we have asked acceleration of blocks and tension in the string. The following short-cut method can be used for simple pulley devices (blocks connected have same acceleration):

Acceleration, $a = \frac{\text{unbalanced load}}{\text{total mass of the system}}$

Load effect : If block moves vertically it will be mg.
If block moves horizontally it will be zero.
If block moves on inclined it will be $mg \sin\theta$.

For tension in the string : Take total mass hanging from the string, if they move up, then

$$T = m_{up}(g + a).$$

And if they move downwards, then

$$T = m_{down}(g - a).$$

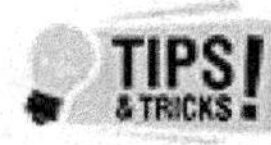

FIG.60: SHORT NOTES FOR NEET PHYSICS

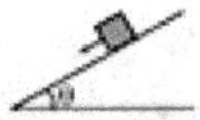

Important Orders (Inorganic + Organic Chemistry)

- Hydrogen bonding > Ion-dipole force > Dipole-dipole force > Dipole-induced Dipole force

- $I < Br < Cl < F$ (Reactivity)

- $3°$ Alcohol > $2°$ Alcohol > $1°$ Alcohol (Reactivity)

- $CH_3OH > 1°$ Alcohol > $2°$ Alcohol > $3°$ Alcohol

- Carboxylic Acid > phenol > water > Alcohol

- CH_3OH is more acidic than H_2O

- $R-COO- > C_6H_5O^- > OH^-$ $R-O^-$ (stability of anions)

- Aldehydes > ketones

- $HCOH > CH_3CHO > CH_3CH_2CHO$

- $CH_3COCH_3 > CH_3COC_2H_5 > C_2H_5COC_2H_5$

- $HCOOH < CH_3COOH < C_2H_5COOH$ (Boiling points, [100, 118, 141])

- $CH_3CH_2COOH < CH_3CH_2CH_2COOH > CH_3CH_2CH_2CH_2COOH$ (melting points)
  (odd −22°c)　(even −6°c)

- $CH_3COOH > CH_3CH_2COOH$ (Reactivity)

- Aliphatic > Aromatic (except Formic)

- Carboxylic Acid > phenol > water > Alcohol

- Acyl chloride > Anhydride > C.A = Ester > Amide > carboxylate

- $F > Cl > Br > I$ (Nature of substituent)

- $Cl_3 > Cl_2 > Cl$

- Carboxylic Acid > Aldehyde > ketones > Alcohol > Alkane

FIG.61 SHORT NOTES FOR JEE CHEMISTRY

Group 13

$$B + HNO_3 \xrightarrow[\Delta]{H_2SO_4} H_3BO_3 + NO_2$$

$$B + KOH \xrightarrow{\Delta} K_3BO_3 + H_2$$

$$B + NaCO_3 + NaNO_3 \longrightarrow Na_3BO_3 + NaNO_3 + CO_2$$

$$B + O_2 \longrightarrow B_2O_3 \qquad B + N_2 \longrightarrow BN \qquad B + C \longrightarrow B_4C$$

$$H_3BO_3 \xrightarrow{\Delta} HBO_2 \xrightarrow{\Delta} B_2O_3$$
$$(\text{orthoboric acid}) \qquad (\text{metaboric acid}) \qquad (\text{Boric anhydride})$$

$$B_2O_3 + NaOH \longrightarrow NaBO_2 + H_2O$$
$$(\text{Sodium metaborate})$$

$$B_2O_3 + CuO \longrightarrow Cu(BO_2)_2$$

$$B_2O_3 + CoO \longrightarrow Co(BO_2)_2$$

$$Na_2B_4O_7 \cdot 10H_2O \xrightarrow{\Delta} Na_2B_4O_7 + H_2O$$
$$\downarrow \Delta$$
$$NaBO_2 + B_2O_3$$

$$H_3BO_3 + Na_2CO_3 \longrightarrow Na_2B_4O_7 + CO_2 + H_2O$$

$$B_2H_6 + H_2O \longrightarrow B(OH)_3 + H_2$$

$$BF_3 + LiAlH_4 \longrightarrow B_2H_6 + LiF + AlF_3$$

$$BF_3 + NaH \longrightarrow B_2H_6 + NaF$$

$$NaBH_4 + I_2 \longrightarrow B_2H_6 + NaI + H_2$$

$$B_2H_6 + NH_3 \xrightarrow{\Delta} B_3N_3H_6 + H_2$$
$$(\text{Borazine})$$

FIG.62: SHORT NOTES FOR NEET CHEMISTRY

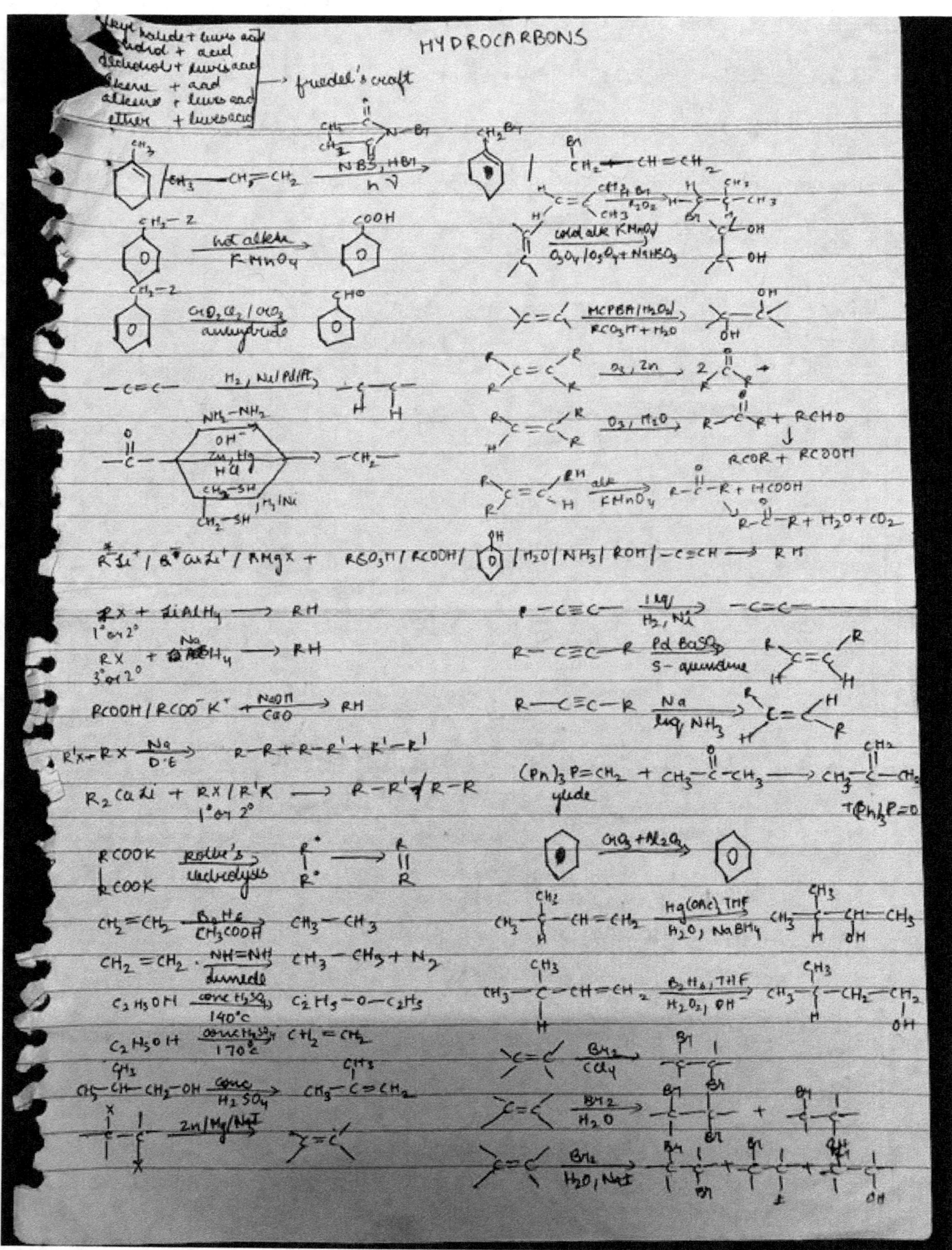

FIG.63: SHORT NOTES FOR NEET CHEMISTRY

Conic Sections- Algebra

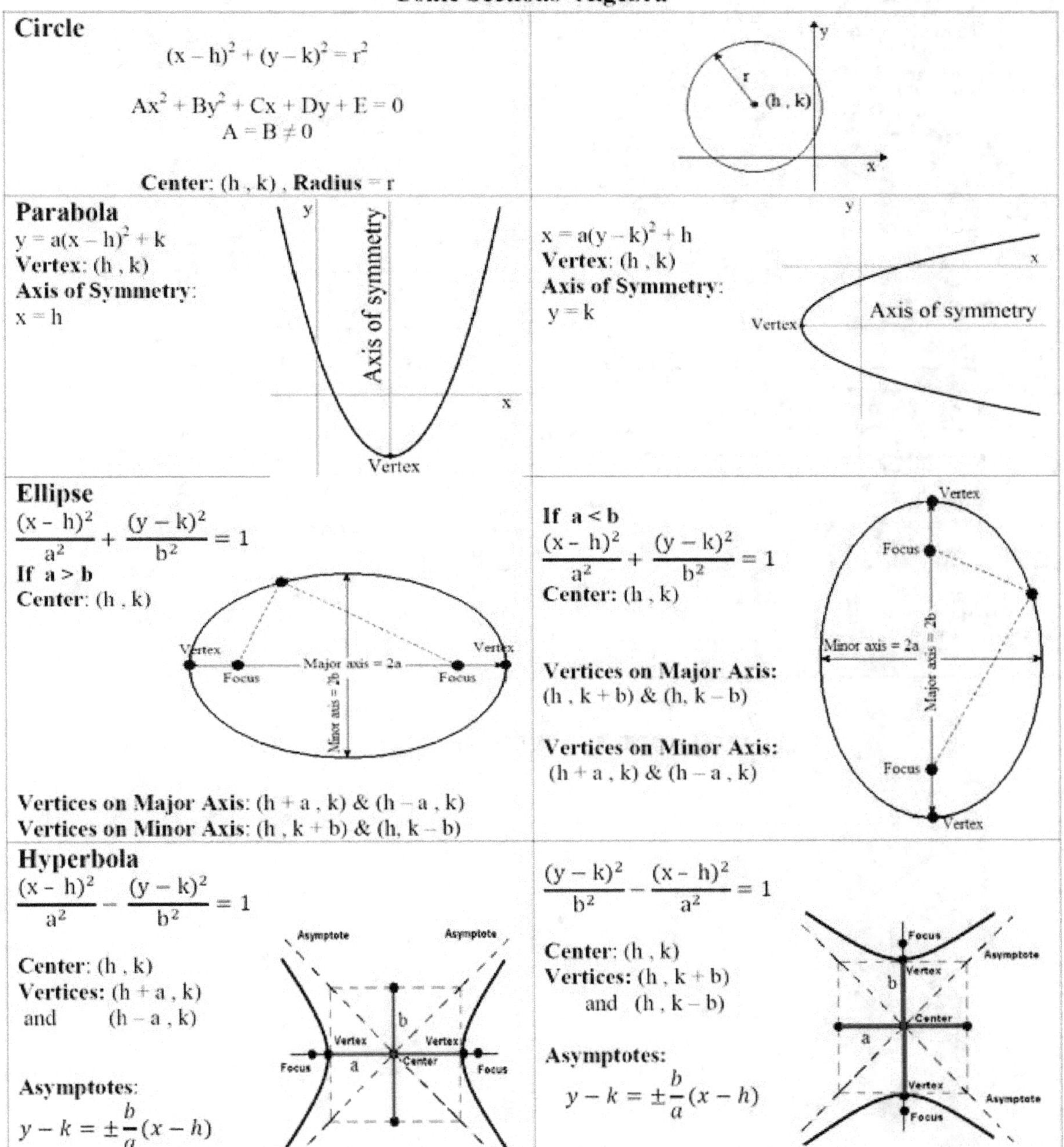

FIG.64: SHORT NOTES FOR JEE MATHEMATICS

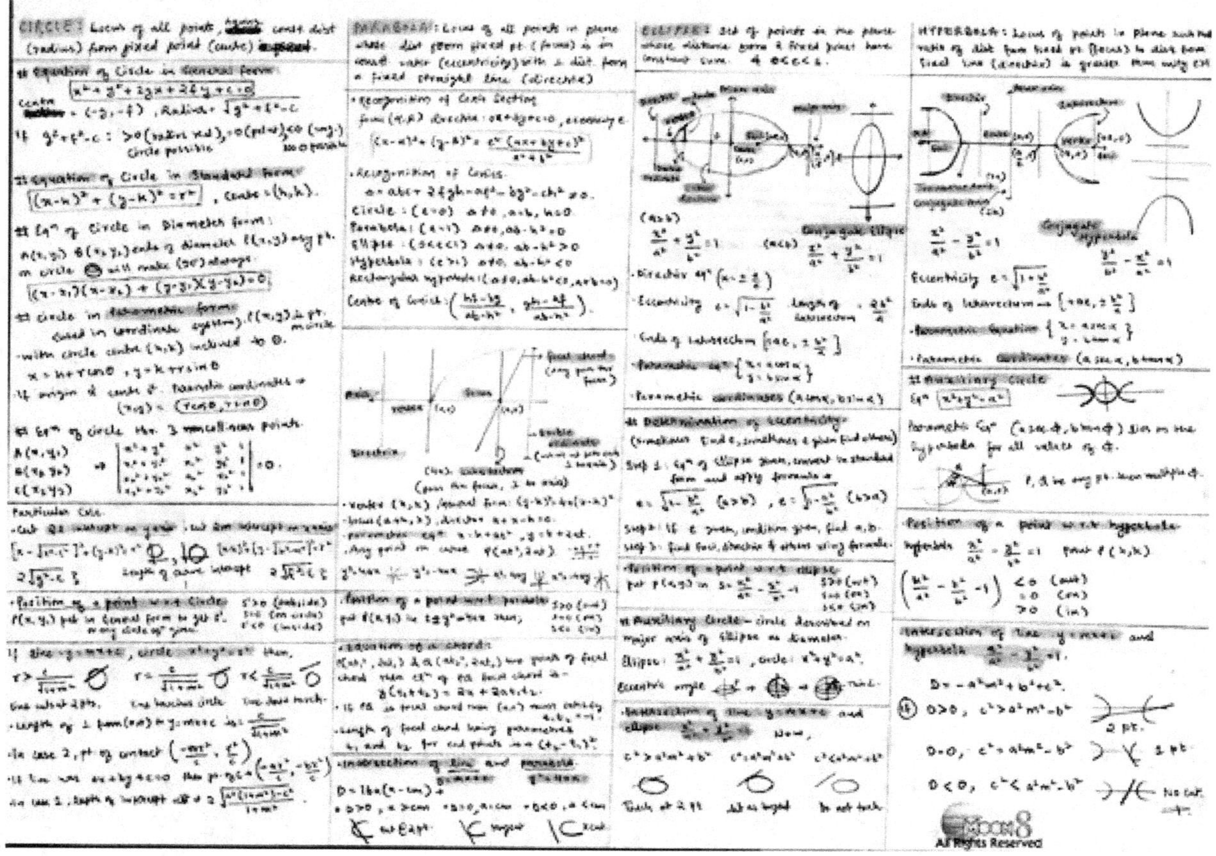

FIG.65: SHORT NOTES FOR JEE MATHEMATICS

INORGANIC TRENDS

GROUP-1 (Alkali Metals)

#1) PROPERTIES

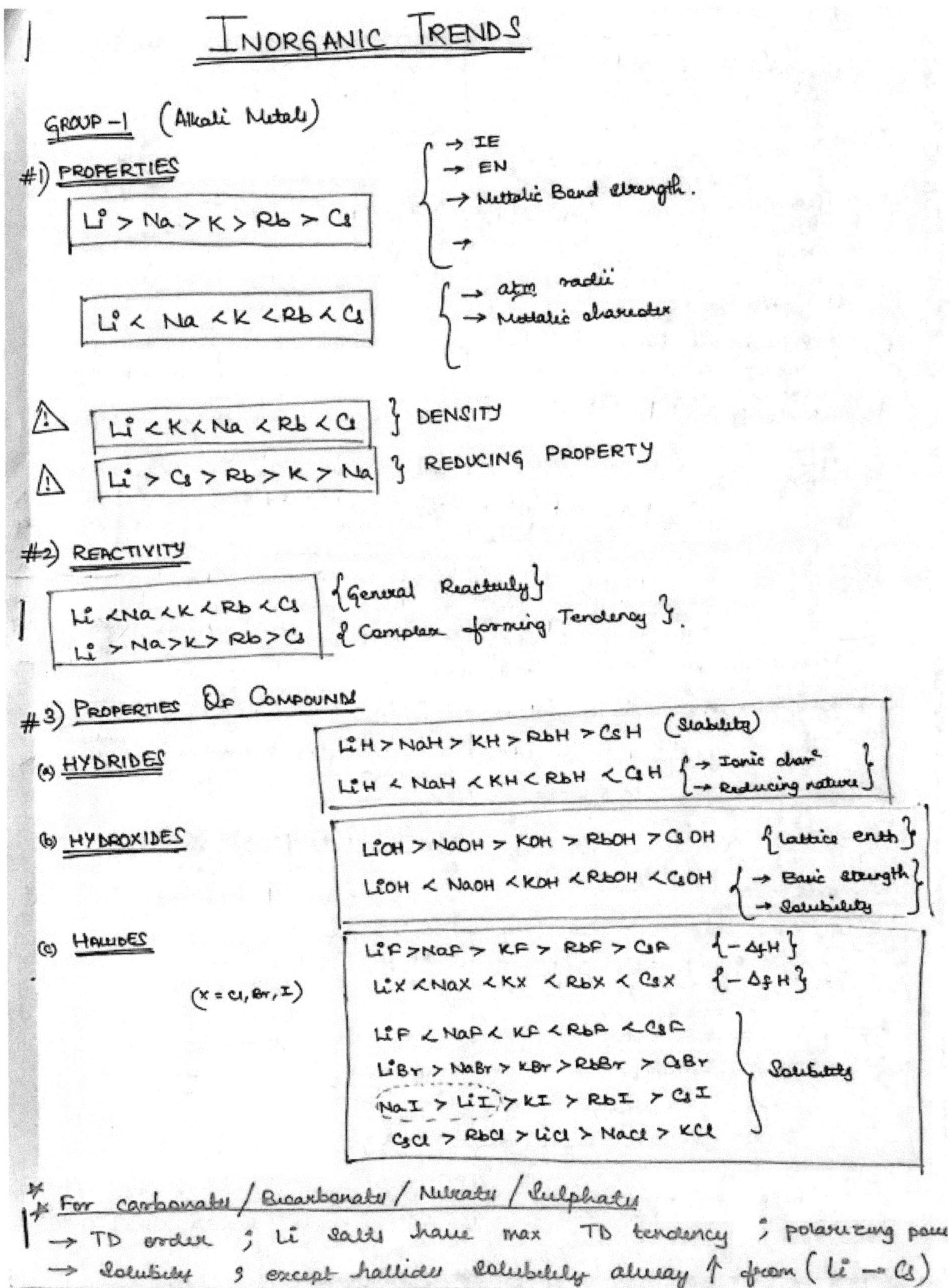

✳ For carbonate / Bicarbonate / Nitrate / Sulphate
→ TD order ; Li salts have max TD tendency ; polarizing power
→ Solubility ; except halides solubility always ↑ from (Li → Cs)

FIG-66: SHORT NOTES FOR NEET CHEMSITRY

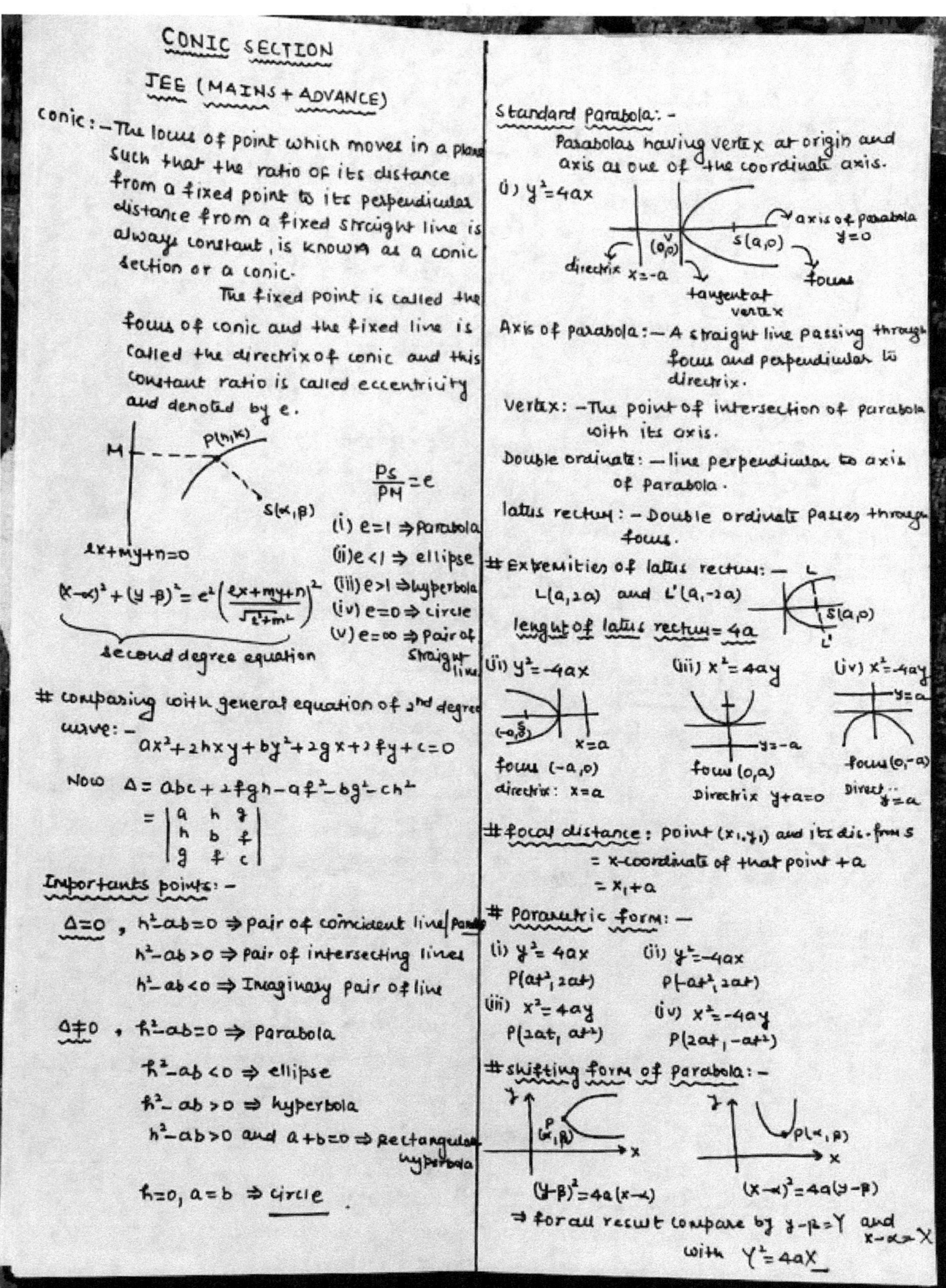

FIG-67: SHORT NOTES FOR JEE MATHEMATICS

SSCResult.in

Maths
Shortcut Tricks
For
Competitive
Exam

84. (i) Area of $\Delta = \dfrac{1}{2}$ bc SinP where $\angle P = \angle QPR$

(ii) Area of $\Delta = \dfrac{1}{2}$ ac SinQ

(iii) Area of $\Delta = \dfrac{1}{2}$ ab SinR

85. $CosP = \dfrac{b^2 + c^2 - a^2}{2bc}$, $CosQ = \dfrac{a^2 + c^2 - b^2}{2ac}$,

$CosR = \dfrac{a^2 + b^2 - c^2}{2ab}$

86. **Sine Rule** : $\dfrac{a}{SinP} = \dfrac{b}{SinQ} = \dfrac{c}{SinR}$

FIG-68: SHORT NOTES FOR SSC

MATH CONIC WORKSHEET

CIRCLE

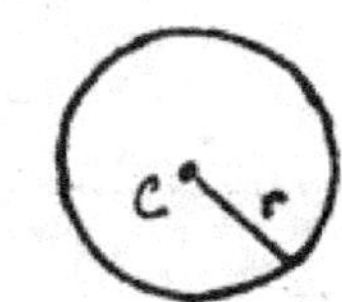

Equation $(x-h)^2 + (y-k)^2 = r^2$

Conic $Ax^2 + By^2 + Cx + Dy + F = 0$

$A = B$ (neither is zero)

Center $= (h, k)$

radius $= r$

PARABOLA

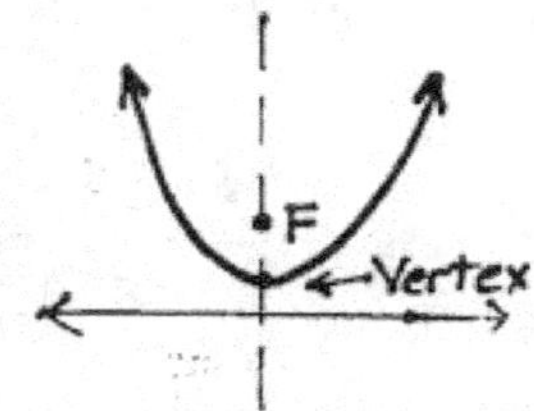

Equation $y = \frac{1}{4p}(x-h)^2 + K$

Vertex: (h, K)

Focus: $(h, K+p)$

Directrix: $y = K-p$

Conic $A = 0$ or $B = 0$

VERTICAL

Equation $x = \frac{1}{4p}(y-K)^2 + h$

Vertex (h, K)

Focus: $(h+p, K)$

Directrix: $x = h-p$

ELLIPSE

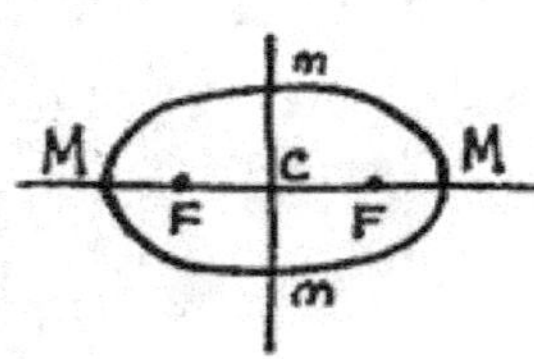

$A \neq B$ but $A > 0$, $B > 0$

Equation $\frac{(x-h)^2}{a^2} + \frac{(y-K)^2}{b^2} = 1$

center: (h, K)

Foci: $(h + \sqrt{a^2-b^2}, K)$, $(h - \sqrt{a^2-b^2}, K)$

Major extrema: $(h+a, k)$, $(h-a, k)$

minor extrema: $(h, K+b)$, $(h, K-b)$

same, but $b > a$

Center: (h, K)

Foci: $(h, K+\sqrt{b^2-a^2})$, $(h, K-\sqrt{b^2-a^2})$

Major: $(h, K+b)$, $(h, K-b)$

minor: $(h+a, K)$, $(h-a, K)$

HYPERBOLA

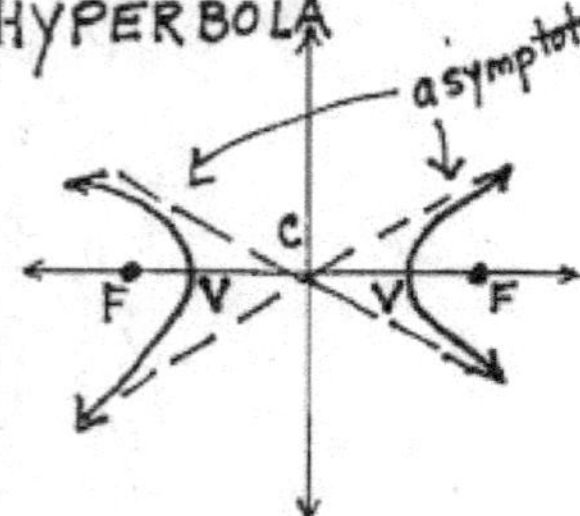

Equation $\frac{(x-h)^2}{a^2} - \frac{(y-K)^2}{b^2} = 1$

center: (h, K)

Vertices: $(h+a, K)$, $(h-a, K)$

Foci: $(h+\sqrt{a^2+b^2}, K)$, $(h-\sqrt{a^2+b^2}, K)$

Asymptotes: $y-K = \pm\frac{b}{a}(x-h)$

$\frac{(y-k)^2}{b^2} - \frac{(x-h)^2}{a^2}$

Center: (h, K)

Vertices: $(h, K+b)$, $(h, K-b)$

Foci: $(h, K+\sqrt{a^2+b^2})$, $(h, K-\sqrt{a^2+b^2})$

Asymptotes: $y-K = \pm\frac{a}{b}(x-h)$

FIG.69: SHORT NOTES FOR CLASS 12 MATHEMATICS

CHAPTER EIGHT

MIND MAPS

After making short notes its necessary to develop mind maps so that you can remember and retain most of the information in exam.

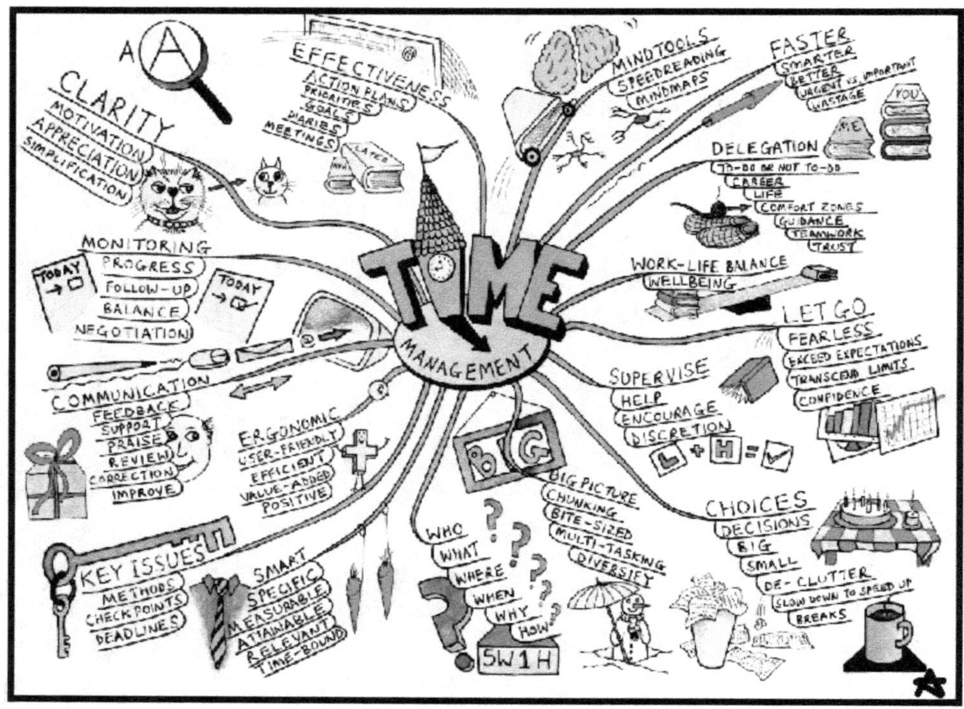

FIG.70:MIND MAPS

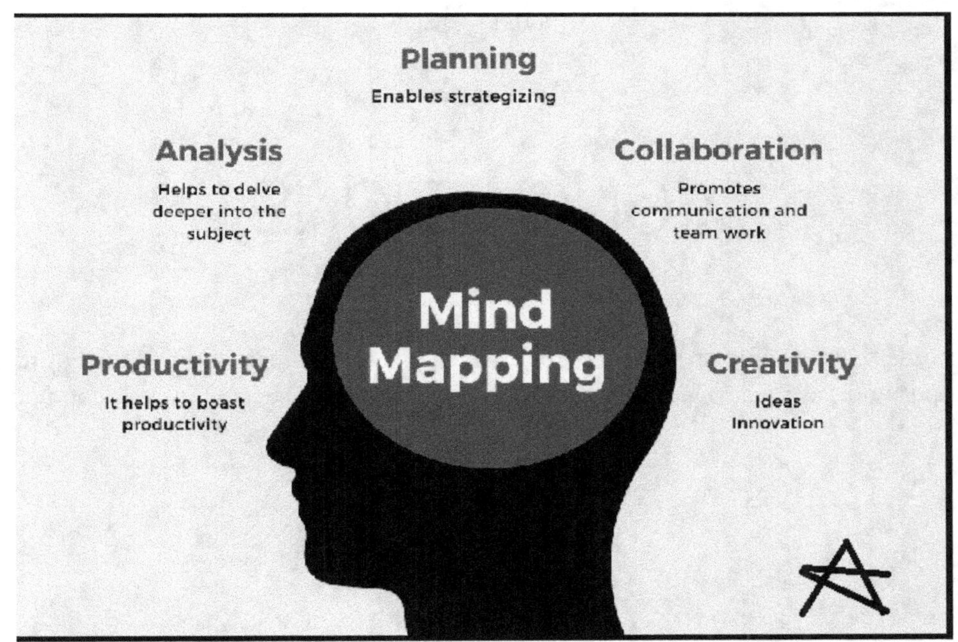

FIG.71:MIND MAPS

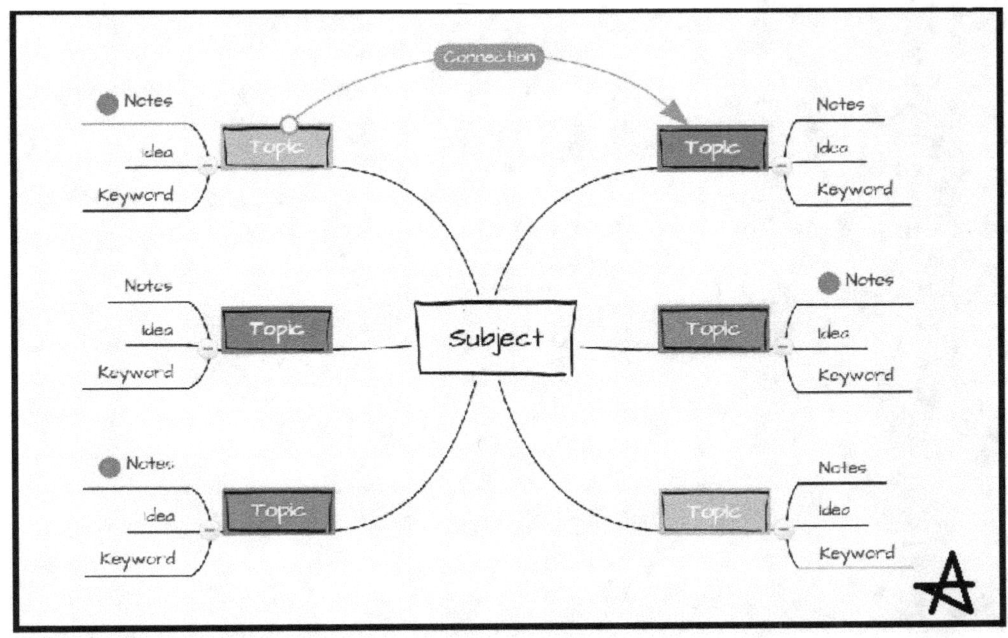

FIG.72:MIND MAPS

CHAPTER NINE

CONCLUSIONS

Hence we can conclude that develpig notes for competitive exams is an integral part of the entire preparation.Make sure to develop proper notes as mentioned earlier and achieve remarkable success in your competitive exam.

we have tried our best to keep this book error free.However if reasders find any error they ar requested to send us the corrections or any feedback at acharyavishvendra@gmail.com